Japanese weapons

An Anthology

- horse & bow
- short staff
- archery
- halberd
- test cutting

An anthology of articles from the
Journal of Asian Martial Arts
Compiled by Michael A. DeMarco, M.A.

Disclaimer

Please note that the authors and publisher of this book are not responsible in any manner whatsoever for any injury that may result from practicing the techniques and/or following the instructions given within. Since the physical activities described herein may be too strenuous in nature for some readers to engage in safely, it is essential that a physician be consulted prior to training.

All Rights Reserved

No part of this publication, including illustrations, may be reproduced or utilized in any form or by any means, electronic or mechanical, including photocopying, recording, or by any information storage and retrieval system (beyond that copying permitted by sections 107 and 108 of the US Copyright Law and except by reviewers for the public press), without written permission from Via Media Publishing Company.

Warning: Any unauthorized act in relation to a copyright work may result in both a civil claim for damages and criminal prosecution.

Copyright © 2020
by Via Media Publishing Company

Articles in this anthology were originally published in the *Journal of Asian Martial Arts*. Listed according to the table of contents for this anthology:

Jones, D. (1992), Vol. 1 No. 1, pp. 68-71
Amdur, E. (1995), Vol. 4 No. 1, pp. 32-49
Hesselink, R. (1993), Vol. 4 No. 4, pp. 40-49
Polland, R. (1997), Vol. 6 No. 3, pp. 88-95
Klens-Bigman, K. (2001), Vol. 10 No. 1, pp. 74-83
Symmes, E. (2010), Vol. 19 No. 1, pp. 54-9
Ward, P. (2013), Vol. 22 No. 1, pp. 60-79

Cover illustration
Guro Tokimune prepares to avenge the death of his father with a night attack. Print by Taiso Yoshitoshi, 1885. ⓢPublic domain.

Print Edition
ISBN-13: 9798639868412

www.viamediapublishing.com

contents

iv **Preface**
by Michael DeMarco, M.A.

CHAPTERS

1 **Testing for Shodan in Japan: Kyudo and Jodo**
by David Jones, Ph.D.

7 **The Development and History of the Naginata,**
by Ellis Amdur, M.A.

29 **The Warrior's Prayer:**
Tokugawa Yoshimune Revives the Yabusame Ceremony
by Reinier H. Hesselink, Ph.D.

41 **Hikiotoshi Uchi Kihon: Jodo's Pull and Drop Strike**
by Rick Polland, B.A.

49 **My Heart is the Target: Interview with Archer Shibata Kanjuro**
by Deborah Klens-Bigman, Ph.D.

61 **Is There a Warrior Within?**
by Edwin Symmes, B.A.

67 **Sword-Cutting Practice of Feudal Japan:**
Anatomical Considerations of Tameshigiri
by Peter J. Ward, Ph.D.

88 **Index**

preface

This anthology presents an assortment of seven articles from the *Journal of Asian Martial Arts* that deal with Japanese weaponry: archery, short staff, naganita polearm, and test cutting (*tamashigiri*) with the long sword. A few articles are highly academic and others are easier reading, based on interviews or actual practice.

Three chapters place a focus on archery and the related formalities of ritual and practice. Two of these discuss the uniqueness of Japanese *kyudo*—the Way of the Bow. As kyudo is a martial art practiced as a *do* or "spiritual way," the authors emphasize the meditative aspects. Dr. Hesselink's chapter differs in that his work details the art of archery performed at full-gallop on horseback.

In the first chapter, Dr. Jones discusses his personal experience in Japan while testing for blackbelt in jodo—the Way of the short staff. In another chapter, Rick Polland points out aspects of solo short staff practice and how it also applies with an opponent.

Ellis Amdur's chapter dives into great detail on the history and evolution of the naganita—a bladed polearm ustilized over many centuries in Japanese warfare and later also as a *do* practice with individual spiritual cultivation as its primary objective. The beauty of naganita blades are no less intrincally interesting than the highly respected making and use of Japanese swords.

Tameshigiri—test cutting—is the topic of the final chapter. Utilizing the Swiss Visual Human technology, Dr. Ward analized sixteen major cuts that were often used by the samurai against their opponents. In the past, test cutters would use human cadavers to see exactly how sword cuts affected particular body parts, e.g., neck, torso, wrist, etc. Each area attacked could be rated according to the difficulty of each cut. How does the composition of the body (thickness of bone, muscle tissue, cartledge, etc.) affect the skillfull execution of the blade? The questions and answers that arise while reading this chapter provide great insight into the use of all bladed weapons.

Although the chapters in this anthology discuss archery, the short staff, mounted archery, the naginata and test cutting, there is a common theme: the importance of these to Japanese martial traditions.

Michael A. DeMarco, Publisher
Santa Fe, New Mexico, May 2020

chapter 1

Testing for Shodan in Japan Kyudo and Jodo

by David E. Jones, Ph.D.

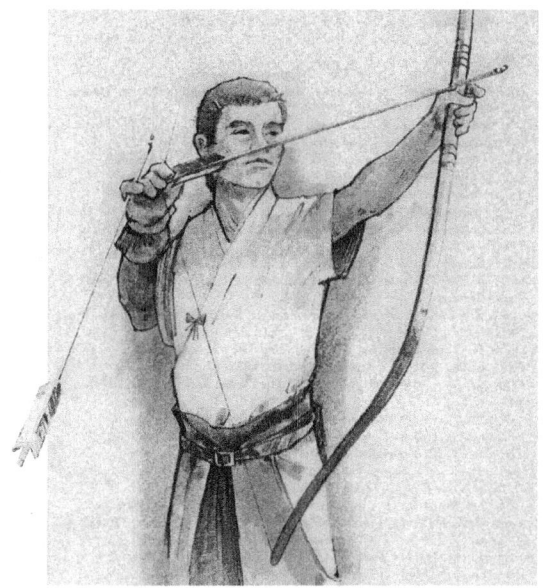

Illustration by Raymond Copper.

From March 1988, to April 1989, I lived and worked in Fukuoka, Japan, as a Visiting Fulbright Professor at two Japanese universities. During my free time, I concentrated on the study of aikido, kyudo, jodo, and the Zen shakuhatchi of the Komuso sect of Fuke Zen. At the end of one year, I was fortunate to be asked to test for *shodan* (first degree blackbelt) in *kyudo* (archery) and Muso-ryu jodo (short-staff fighting methods). In this chapter, I would like to describe the nature of testing procedures for the All Japan Kyudo Federation and the Shindo Muso-ryu Jodokai.

To move from beginner to first degree blackbelt in one year is not at all typical in *budo* (the warrior way), but I was not a beginner when I went to Japan. I had twenty years of martial arts training behind me, a nidan rank in Sakugawa Koshiki Shorinji-ryu Karatedo, and sandan rank in Ueshiba-ryu Aikido. The lessons learned from karatedo and aikido training in the USA. were automatically applied when I entered the archery and staff fighting dojo in Japan. Proper attitude toward teachers and seniors, centering, relaxation, civilized demeanor, intense training style, consciousness of posture and stance, elegance and dignity of movement, and a constant awareness of respect for all things and all people around me, coupled with the study and practice of karatedo kata and the jo and boken of aikido, separated me from the beginning Japanese students at the outset.

I must thank my instructors: Mr. Edward Baker (aikido), Mr. Thomas Cauley (karate), Mr. Chan Poi (Wah Lum gongfu and taijiquan), and Mitsugi Saotome Shihan (Headmaster of the Aikido Schools of Ueshiba) for establishing in me patterns and attitudes of martial arts training behavior which were recognized as correct by the teachers I confronted in Japan.

My Japanese budo sensei were truly amazing people. I received instruction in kyudo from Asakuma Shihan (master teacher), three times All Japan Women's Kyudo Champion, and recent recipient of the rank of *hanshi* (ninth degree blackbelt). My jodo teacher was Torinaga Shihan, an eighth degree blackbelt and a direct descendent of Muso Gonnosuke, founder of the Muso-ryu and the only man ever to fight to a draw the famous Japanese swordsman Miyamoto Musashi.

Testing for Shodan in Kyudo

About eleven months into my kyudo training, I was asked by Asakuma Shihan to test for *nikyu* (second degree brown belt) at an upcoming examination which would draw together all the kyudo master teachers of Kyushu (the southernmost island of Japan) and several hundred students. In preparation, I focused on the basic shooting kata, which involved shooting two arrows over a 28-meter range at a target about the size of a barrel head. The arrows are custom made to the student. In my case I was shooting arrows that were 42-inches long with a composite bamboo bow (about a 70 pound pull) that when strung stood over seven feet. The basic shooting kata began with very precisely prescribed steps used to enter the shooting area, a ritualized approach to the shooting line, a prearranged method of fitting and raising the arrow, shooting, kneeling to refit the second arrow, rising in posture, shooting again, and leaving the shooting area, again with each step fixed in the traditional kata routine. I practiced about eight hours a week, and in each two-hour session I shot about thirty to forty arrows, hitting the target two or three times if I was having a good day.

The test was held in the nearby town of Agi at the foot of an old castle. There were hundreds of Japanese archery students present, and I was the only foreign male. We were sent onto the shooting floor in groups of four. At a long table against the wall facing the shooters sat the judges' panel composed of about seven venerable old kyudo shihans. When my turn came to shoot, I could see hundreds of Japanese kyudo students move toward the fences on the side of the shooting range to see the tall *gaijin* (foreigner) shoot, a sight few of them had ever seen in that part of Japan. I was aware of them and also aware of the penetrating gaze of the shihans who sat about five feet in front of me. However, as we all know, kata training enables the student to enter a quiet and private space. My first shot hit the center of the target. I wasn't aware at the moment how important that hit was. I later found that no other student testing for the upper kyu ranks that day had hit the target. I was the only one. My second shot came close but missed. I completed my kata, rose and left the shooting area.

As my teachers and fellow students were congratulating me, a senior student, a fifth dan, who spoke some English came up to me and asked me to follow him to the examination room. I had not heard of an "examination room" in my preparation for the day's testing. When I asked him what was to happen next, he said, "You hit target. You must now test for shodan." When I asked him what the shodan test would be, he said, "Now you must answer some questions."

The rank of shodan is awarded if the testing panel judges that your kata is correct, showing "poignancy and internal kiai," as one kyudoka put it, if you hit the target and if you pass a written test. The written test, the task that faced me in the examination room, consisted of three questions. The first question asked to describe the history of kyudo; the second question, to select one of the postures in the shooting kata and to describe it in detail; the third question, required an essay describing the goal of budo training. I was prepared for this test because I had misunderstood earlier instructions and thought that these questions would be asked of me for advancement to nikyu. Furthermore, reading on the nature and philosophy of the martial arts as well as discussions with fellow budoka while in the US enabled me to tell the Japanese teachers what they wanted to hear concerning the spiritual nature of budo training and its goal of creating a peaceful society. Several Japanese students did not pass to the shodan rank because in their written test they had described the goal of budo training as the creation of physical strength and fighting ability, a type of response which one budo sensei referred to as "unseasoned and immature."

The "wrong" answer would stress the acquisition of physical strength and fighting ability.

I learned an important lesson that day when I returned from my successful written test and was told I was now a shodan. When Asakuma Sensei congratulated me, I said "I was just lucky." I was! There were days at the dojo when I shot forty arrows and never even came close to hitting the target. However, when my comments were translated to her, she frowned at me and the tone of her comments told me I was being scolded for something. She was telling me that saying I was merely lucky was an insult to her teaching. I had hit the target because of her training! I had hit the target because it was my karma to hit the target at that place and at that time! I was there for a reason! There is no luck! I was reminded of the old Zen saying, "A snowflake does not fall in the wrong place."

Testing for Shodan in Jodo
Shindo Muso-ryu jodo is based on an historic combat that took place between Muso Gonnosuke and Miyamoto Musashi in northern Kyushu in the early to mid-1600s in the vicinity of Dazaifu. Muso with his newly developed jo art stood against the two-sword style of the great Musashi. The major heart of the style that emerged from this encounter is characterized by kata in which a swordsman confronts a practitioner of the Muso style of *jo*, or "short-staff." At higher levels, the Muso-ryu also teaches a variety of "weighted chain" weapons used in defense against swords, as well as numerous take-downs, pins, nerve attacks, etc.

Jodo training begins with the basic blocks, parries, strikes, thrusts, and stances which characterize the style. The jo techniques taught in aikido schools are almost exactly the same as those found in jodo, except in jodo the audible kiai is employed, the student is taught to stare intently, without blinking, into the eyes of the attacker as a means to intimidate and control the opponent, and the strikes and blows of the jo actually contact the body of the student during training. I found the gaze of the upper level jodo dans to be unbelievably powerful and immobilizing.

Testing for shodan is possible when the student has "mastered" the basic techniques of the jo as well as the twelve *seitei-kata* (standard fighting forms). The kata begin with simple forms involving only two or three techniques and advances by graded steps to the twelfth in the series which involves about thirty techniques. The katas are named *Tsuki Zue* (Standing Stick); *Suigetsu* (Moon in the Water); *Ran Ai* (Harmony Out of Chaos); etc.

As with kyudo, the jodo testing situation involved several hundred students from all over the Kyushu area. It was held in the Budokan (House of the Warrior Way) in Fukuoka, Japan. The shihan of jodo sat behind a long table with Otofuji Shihan, the headmaster of the style. Before the test, Otofuji Shihan, now elderly and barely able to walk, addressed the students lined up for the testing and stressed the importance of "sincere effort," "brightness of spirit," "manly behavior", and "citizenship" as the "heart of jodo."

The shodan test allowed the students to select five of the seitei-katas to perform although we were not told this until minutes before our name was called to approach the testing area. Fortunately, I had the assistance of Ogata Sensei, a seventh dan, who played the part of the swordsman. I appreciated the old samurai maxim that one should be grateful for an excellent opponent. Ogata Sensei's spirited and precise sword attacks made my job easier.

We went out onto the Budokan floor in sets of four. In turn we called out the name of our kata and proceeded with our demonstration. I started with about the third most difficult kata just to see how I would do with Ogata Sensei. When I became aware that his precision was making me look good, I called out the top four most difficult kata to complete my remaining requirements for testing. Again, as with kyudo, my testing attracted a crowd of spectators, but after almost a year in Kyushu I had become used to drawing a crowd.

When I left the testing area, I was directed to another part of the Budokan for the written test. The format was the same as for the kyudo shodan written test. I was asked to discuss the history of the style, describe one of the seitei-katas in detail, and conclude with an essay on the merits of jodo training. Again, the "right" answer had to do with what Otofuji Shihan had said at the beginning of the testing session and the "wrong" answer would stress the acquisition of physical strength and fighting ability. It must be noted, of course that strength, courage and combat ability are high priorities of budo training, but they are never considered the most important goals to seek. They come as automatic accompaniment to training carried out at more lofty levels of consciousness, and it is that higher level that the budo sensei want to hear about and see reflected in behavior.

It intrigued me to discover that, in the case of many of the Japanese jodo students, as with some of the kyudo students, the point of budo training was totally misunderstood. Most of the beginner Japanese budo students apparently do not read books on the subject, and only rarely, as in the case of Otofuji Shihan's address to the testing jodo students, do the budo sensei explain the essential point of budo training to them. I found myself in the somewhat embarrassing situation of being promoted to shodan in jodo while better physical specimens than I were held back. The only difference was that I had the right response to the written test. The Japanese budo sensei place great stress on the mature thought processes and civilized behavior of their advanced students.

I feel very grateful for the opportunity to train in Japan and to experience the first-hand teaching of hanshi-level teachers of the martial way. I learned many physical techniques from the Japanese aikido, kyudo and jodo instructors, and had many penetrating insights into my own psyche and nature, but I also found that my formative training in the deeper meaning of budo coming from instructors in America was what separated me from the other "beginner" students in the two dojos in which I trained. The teachers in the United States who had created the foundation of my understanding of budo enabled me to find success in Japan.

A snowflake does not

fall in the wrong place.

– Zen proverb

chapter 2

The Development and History of the Naginata

by Ellis Amdur, M.A.

Ukiyo-e print by Tsukioka Yoshitoshi showing a samurai deflecting arrows with a naginata. Dated 1869.
ⓢ *Public domain. United States Library of Congress; digital ID cph.3g08655*

Origins

Up until the ninth century, Japanese warfare was characterized by the use of three major weapons: the bow-and-arrow and the straight sword, used by mounted warriors and those on foot, and the *hoko*, a spear with a socketed spearhead, used exclusively by foot soldiers. Combat techniques underwent radical change in the mid-Heian period (794-1185 C.E.) with the proliferation of the curved cavalry sword known as the *tachi*. This change corresponded to the rise of the aristocratic warrior class (*bushi*). With tactics honed in battles on the frontier with unassimilated aboriginal groups and internecine warfare among clans, the *bushi* became some of the most effective cavalry fighters the world has ever known. The *tachi*, relatively light and deeply curved, could still be used to thrust and stab, but it was more usually used as a weapon to cut and slash.

As cavalry tactics became more effective, foot soldiers began to receive weapons more adequate to counter them. One might imagine that the spear, with centuries of use behind it, was more than adequate to the task, but the *hoko* was abandoned in this period and replaced with other weapons. It is unknown why this happened. Donn Draeger suggests that the *hoko*, with their socketed spearheads, were rather poorly mounted on the shafts of the weapon and often came off when a stabbed individual's musculature clamped down on the spearhead that had so sorely wounded him (Draeger, 1974: 73). It may also be that warriors became so enthralled with the devastating power of the *tachi* that they made similar use of long weapons and abandoned weapons which specialized in the thrust rather than the cut. At any rate, the use of the *hoko* declined at this time and spear fighting largely disappeared for several hundred years.

At the same time, Japanese warriors (both *bushi* and warrior monks known as *sohei*) began fighting with a large glaive, a curved blade mounted on a stout oak shaft. These weapons were known as *naginata*. The characters that were first used to write its name were *zhang dao*, which means "long sword."

We have little systematic knowledge of the origins and development of the naginata. The warrior class was an elite and, for the most part, it is the elite who are remembered in history. Therefore, it is their weaponry which has been most studied. The elite of Japan were the horse-riding *bushi*, not their retainers on foot who utilized the naginata. Nonetheless, even the origins of the *tachi* are shrouded in mystery. Culture myths assert that the almost god-like sword-smith, Amakuni, created the first known *tachi*, called the *kogarasu-maru*, developing it from the straight, single-edged cavalry swords of the late Nara period or very early Heian period (approximately 700). However, many scholars believe that the *tachi* may, in fact, have been introduced several hundred years later (Ogasawara [1970]; Draeger-Warner [1982]). If the origins of the *tachi*, the weapon of the elite, are unknown, imagine how much more inaccessible are the origins of the naginata, a weapon of common fighters, whose deeds are mostly recorded *en masse* and not as the feats of individual heroes.

Up to the thirteenth century, at least, warfare consisted largely of mounted battles or brief "sieges" of lightly fortified or geographically advantageous positions. Sieges were broken quickly by direct attack, infiltration, or the besieged themselves coming out to fight. It was considered shameful to be inactive in the face of aggression. Strategy was usually very simple. Two sides started a battle with a volley of arrows. Then individual combat would begin, often with only one warrior from each side. Finally, the two groups would charge together to fight *en masse*, the mounted warriors with *tachi*, those on foot with both *tachi* and naginata. Most early accounts of the use of naginata refer to it being used behind barricades, to stab and cut at horses. There are few famous naginata fighters whose deeds are recorded. This does not mean that it was not a significant weapon, simply that it was used by low-ranking fighters, who were historically important only insofar as they affected the powerful. The number of dead retainers in a battle might not even be mentioned in the records; that such and such a warrior had his horse cut out from under him surely would be.

Its name, at least, suggests that the naginata was developed from the sword and this is certainly a logical conclusion. Unlike the *hoko* of an earlier era with their socketed spearheads, most naginata, like swords, were fitted to their shaft with a long tang. It is very possible that the first naginata were improvised weapons, *tachi* blades lashed onto a spear shaft (Amdur, 1995). Let us envision a foot-soldier whose *hoko* blade had either broken or slipped off its shaft. This soldier knows that he will soon have to face horse-riding attackers or defend himself behind a barricade. By simply splitting the shaft of his *hoko*, inserting the tang of a *tachi*, lashing it with strong cord, and even using a pick or hand drill to make a hole to insert a peg to affix the blade, he would have a serviceable weapon which would be a threat to both horse and rider. Surely such a weapon must have been effective, for more permanent types of naginata were soon developed with long tang and secure mountings.

There are other "origin theories." Some authorities suggest that the naginata might have developed from a curious Nara period weapon called the *teboko* (hand halberd). There are only five remaining examples of this weapon, which have been preserved in the Shosoin, an Imperial storehouse dating from the Nara era. The *teboko* are about four to five feet long. Each has a uniquely shaped tanged blade. The blades are set in shafts of wood wrapped in cherry bark. The butt end is a thicker, unwrapped portion of the shaft. According to Kashima Susumu, the head of the Tokyo National Museum's section on ancient weaponry, the *teboko* are very light, quite different from the heavy functional *hoko* in the Shosoin collection. He states that the *teboko* do not have the feel of functional weapons.[1]

Some *teboko* blades seem more suitable for chopping or cutting, and other, straighter ones could be used for stabbing. Although the blades are of high quality, no one knows if they were meant to be used in combat or if they were purely ceremonial. The tip and cross-section of each unique blade is identical to that of at least one of the many (functional) swords also preserved in the Shosoin. It is conceivable that the *teboko* were produced for purely artistic reasons and the whimsical variations of the blades as well as the joy of fine craft work.

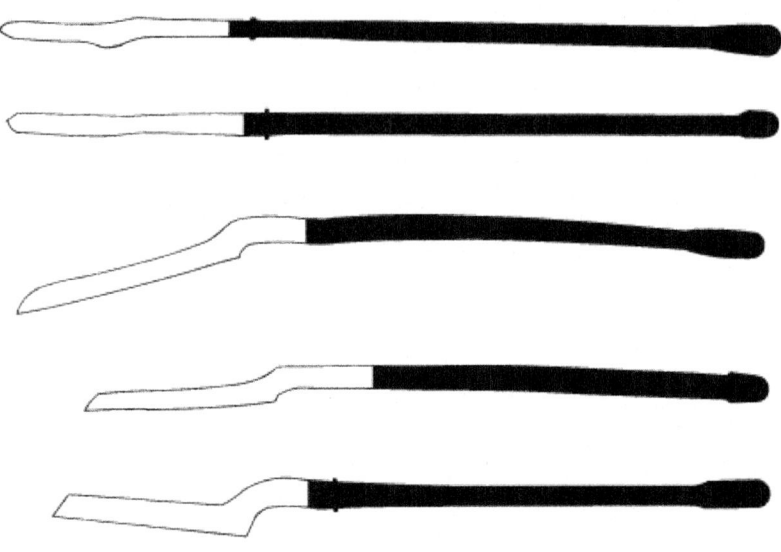

These five teboko, kept in the imperial repository in Nara, are the only known examples of this weapon type. *Illustrated by Shinji Marumori.*

There is no mention of *teboko* under any name in any old records, nor have any other examples been preserved. Though it is possible that some aspects of *teboko* design influenced naginata construction, there is just no evidence to form a conclusion one way or another. However, their existence does show that the Japanese knew how to make tang-bladed, long-shafted weapons at an early date.

It is also suggested that the *guan-dao* or *shang-dao* (Chinese glaive) might have been the prototype of the naginata, and this is an intriguing possibility. The *shang-dao* was widely used in East Asia, spreading as far as Korea and Thailand. In Thailand it was used by mahouts guiding war elephants. It has a characteristic "notch" at the back of the blade, used to catch and break the blade of an enemy. This notch has been retained in every country to which the *shang-dao* is known to have spread, but no Japanese blade is shaped in this manner.

At Hulao Pass, Lü Bu fighting the three brothers:
Liu Bei (swords), Guan Yu (*shang-dao*), and Zhang Fei (spear).
From a print from the *Romance of the Three Kingdoms*. Public domain.

Japan's period of greatest contact with China was between 552 and 866 (Reischauer, 1947). This is the period right before the development of both the *tachi* and the naginata. It is quite possible that Japanese smiths used the *shang-dao* as a prototype for their own weapon. However, there is no evidence in records or contemporary pictures of *shang-dao* being used or imported into Japan at this time, nor have any examples been found. This weapon is referred to in several later war chronicles by its Japanese name, *bisento*.[2] The customary method of writing this is *mei jian dao*, which means "eyebrow pointed blade." In one text, the *Taiheiki*, there is a reference to a gigantic *bisento* with a blade and shaft, each five feet long.

The war chronicles, however, are not the best historical source. They were epics memorized and transmitted orally for hundreds of years by blind bards, much like Homer's *Illiad*. The armament in them may come from the time in which these epics were written, not the time which they describe. A comparable Western example would be Mallory's *Le Morte D'Artur*, in which the "knights of the round table" are armed as medieval knights, not in the simple fashion of their Celtic forebearers.

Benkei Battles Minamoto no Yoshitsune at Gojo Bridge.
Date: 12 January 1200. Source: https://data.ukiyo-e.org/mfa/images/sc133746.jpg
Original in color changed to grey scale. *Creative Commons CC BY-SA 4.0*

In addition, influenced like so much of Japanese culture by the Chinese, these chronicles often include stories, plots and weapons lifted from their Chinese predecessors. This is also true of the *musha-e*, pictures of warriors in battle composed largely in the eighteenth and nineteenth centuries, which often show Chinese demigods wielding a variety of weapons, among them the *shang-dao*.

To sum up, then, it is unknown when the Japanese became aware of the *shang-dao* or whether it served as a prototype for the naginata. That there are no examples of this weapon preserved nor any early illustrations of it suggests, at least, that the Japanese first saw it at a relatively late date and recognized it as a "Chinese naginata" rather than the basis of the Japanese weapon.

There is a rather unusual type of weapon, the socketed-blade naginata, which some authorities have suggested as the prototype of all naginata (see page 13-14). They are known as *nata-naginata* (ax-blade naginata) and *tsukushi naginata* (named after a district in Kyushu). The oldest *nata-naginata* had a short, wide blade, measuring as little as eight inches in length. It was attached to the shaft by one or two sockets on the back of the blade. In the *Dai Nippon Naginata-do Kyoden* (1939), it is stated that the *nata-naginata* was a short-shafted tool used to clear brush and trees in mountainous areas. In times of war, the shaft was replaced with a longer one. The *tsukushi naginata* probably developed from this ax-like weapon, but its blade proportions were similar to those of the usual naginata. Very few of these weapons remain and those that do are made of poor quality steel. They were reportedly used as late as the 1500's, but only by the lowest-ranking conscript foot soldiers. It was a poorly balanced instrument with the blade projecting out from the side of the shaft. More important, the shock of impact was focused in the very small area where the blade was fixed to the shaft. It is possible that more than a few warriors found themselves suddenly holding a broken shaft, giving them an unanticipated introduction to the art of stick fighting.

Because of the poor quality of these weapons, few have been preserved and their date of development is unknown. One can certainly speculate that they were a transitional form, inspired by the socket-headed *hoko*, and thus were developed quite early in the Heian period. Given that other scholars have suggested nearly every period since the Heian, we simply do not know when it was developed.

Because of the complete lack of archeological and documentary evidence to the contrary and the fact that a naginata is such an obvious innovation for any warrior people with curved swords to develop, most authorities believe that the naginata is a native Japanese invention.

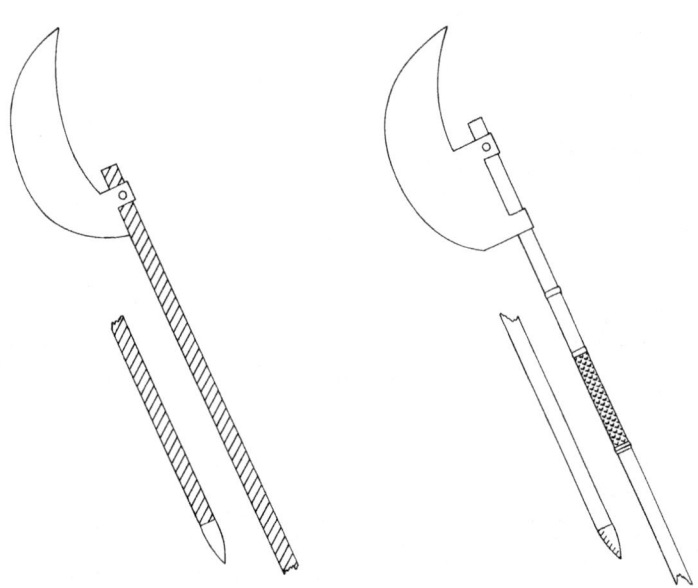

Nata-naginata.
All sketches by Shinji Marumori, derived from the *Dai Nippon Naginata-do Kyoden*.

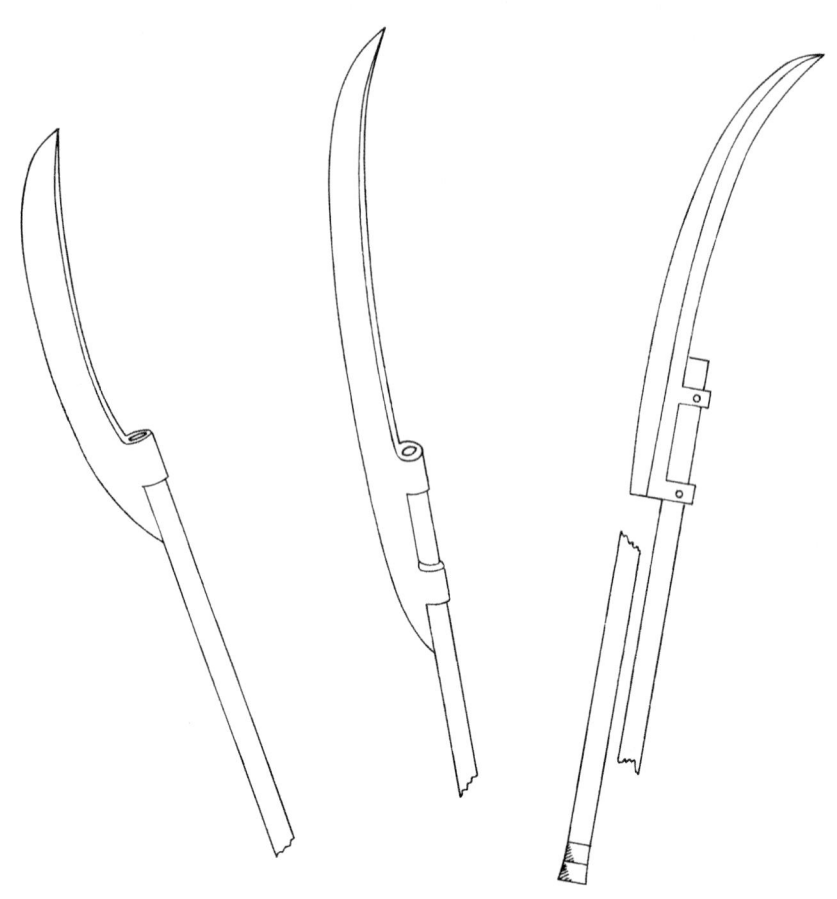

Tsukushi naginata.
All sketches by Shinji Marumori, derived from the *Dai Nippon Naginata-do Kyoden*.

The Weapon

The major type of naginata, the tang-bladed type, appeared sometime in the tenth or eleventh century. It is a weapon of marvelous design. The blades were fashioned with the same laminations of hard and soft steel that were used for sword blades. Although there have been considerable variations in the proportions between the length of the blade and shaft, the length of the entire weapon has always been rather consistent, somewhere between seven and eight feet, with exceptional weapons up to nine feet and a few examples as short as six feet. The weapon's proportions are limited by the proportions of the human body. Too heavy and the weapon will quickly become useless, fatiguing the practitioner and leaving him open to counterattack. Too light and it can be easily blocked and deflected. Too short and it becomes a trivial weapon, similar in range to a sword but more vulnerable due to the greater exposure of the hands to attack. Too long and it is unmaneuverable.

The shaft of the weapon was of red or white Japanese oak (*kashi*), which, with its qualities of flexibility and resistance to both impact and torsion, makes it an ideal material for both hand-held tools and weapons. The shaft was almost always oval in cross-section. This provided maximum strength in the direction of the cut and also gave the user an automatic awareness of the position of the blade. The tang of the blade was very long, sometimes almost as long as the blade itself. Small pieces of wood packed around the tang held it firmly in the slot in the shaft. As Roald Knutson notes in *Japanese Polearms* (1963), when the tang rusts a little it becomes almost impossible to remove. This section of the shaft was bound with cords and then with metal rings. Like swords, bamboo pegs were inserted through the holes in the shaft and tang, and then wrapped in rattan or hemp.

BLADE PARTS

Kissaki – point.
Ha – cutting edge.
Shinogi – ridgehne.
Mune – back edge.
Naginata hi – grooves to reduce weight and improve balance.
Naka go – the tang, inserted into the shaft;
Mekugi Ana – hole for mekugi, a peg used to fix the blade in the shaft.

Mune machi – notch, separating back edge and tang.
Ha machi – notch, separating blade and tang.
Kamuri otoshi – narrowing at center portion of mune (common in blades produced in the muromachi period and after).

[See pages 15 and 16]

SIDE VIEW OF BLADE

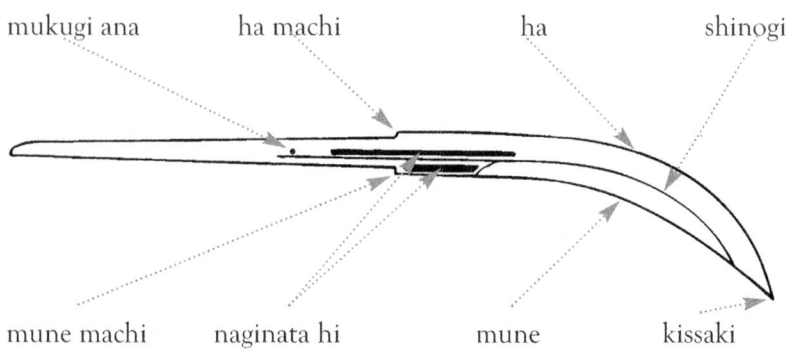

NAGINATA

This rather elaborately mounted naginata is typical of the Edo period (post-1600). Earlier naginata, like the thirteenth century example shown on page 20, were much simpler. All sketches by Shinji Marumori, derived from the *Dai Nippon Naginata-do Kyoden*.

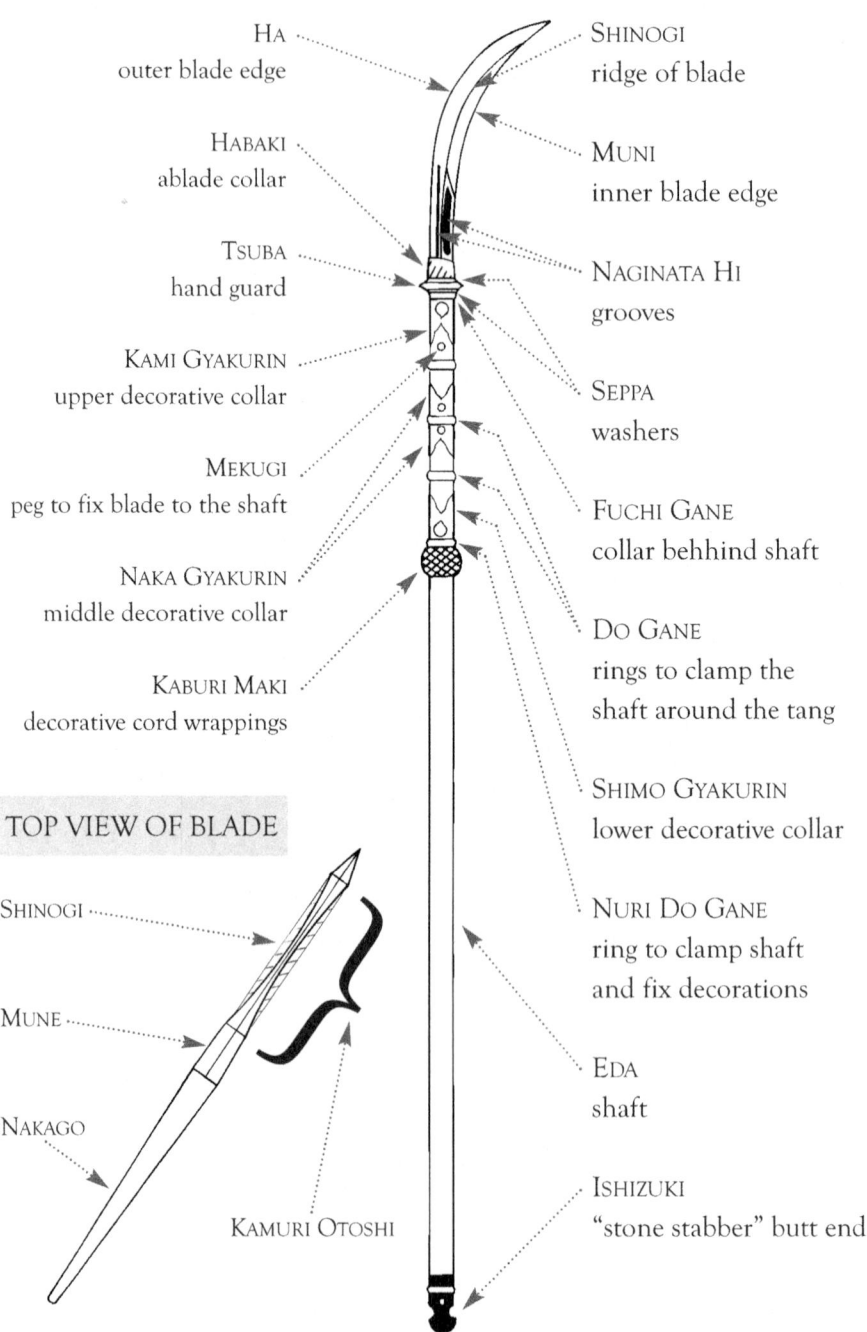

- **HA** — outer blade edge
- **HABAKI** — ablade collar
- **TSUBA** — hand guard
- **KAMI GYAKURIN** — upper decorative collar
- **MEKUGI** — peg to fix blade to the shaft
- **NAKA GYAKURIN** — middle decorative collar
- **KABURI MAKI** — decorative cord wrappings
- **SHINOGI** — ridge of blade
- **MUNI** — inner blade edge
- **NAGINATA HI** — grooves
- **SEPPA** — washers
- **FUCHI GANE** — collar behhind shaft
- **DO GANE** — rings to clamp the shaft around the tang
- **SHIMO GYAKURIN** — lower decorative collar
- **NURI DO GANE** — ring to clamp shaft and fix decorations
- **EDA** — shaft
- **ISHIZUKI** — "stone stabber" butt end

TOP VIEW OF BLADE

- **SHINOGI**
- **MUNE**
- **NAKAGO**
- **KAMURI OTOSHI**

The butt end was capped with a projection of iron or bronze. It was either bluntly pointed or spade-shaped. It has a variety of names, such as *ishizuki* (stone stabber) and *kojiri* (little rear end). It served as a counterweight and protected the shaft from damage, but its most important use was as a means of attack. Users of a naginata would often reverse the weapon, and strike or thrust with the *ishizuki*. This was particularly useful in killing a downed opponent. Cutting effectively at an armored person rolling on the ground or close to one's legs is difficult with a long weapon. Stabbing at the wrong angle could break off the tip of the blade. In addition, with the force of the strike travelling through the person into the ground, it is easy to break the shaft. The *ishizuki* enabled warriors to simply stab downward with all the force of their body. This could be done at close range, the shock being absorbed by the entire shaft. With the combined weight of the heavy weapon and the user, it could smash right through armor. The *ishizuki* greatly increased the variety and range of techniques. A naginata without an *ishizuki* would be only half a weapon.

It is quite difficult to study the changes in the shape of the blade because so few remain. Smiths of different areas favored different designs, and, as far as we know, there was not an orderly progression to a more sophisticated weapon. In addition, by the seventeenth century, the war naginata was regarded as rather old-fashioned. It had been supplanted by other weapons and most people saw little need or value in preserving them. People took their naginata to smiths and had the blades cut and reworked into swords. This was called *naginata naoshi* (naginata reworking).

Because of this, only general statements can be made about the shape of the naginata. No scholar seems to have attempted to categorize blades by geographical area or by small variations in structure and shape. There are simply not enough blades to study.

The naginata blades of the Heian and early Kamakura periods (1185-1333 C.E.) were rather straight. They were about the same width throughout most of the length of the blade. The ridgeline (*shinogi*) went out to the point. Thus, the blades look rather similar to those of swords. Pictures of the Kamakura period show warriors with huge curved naginata. However, no such blades have been found. Larry Bieri (1982) suggests that these dramatic blades are more the product of the artists' imaginations than the smiths' forges, for such a curved blade would be very difficult to make. It addition, such a weapon would be less useful for stabbing and thrusting attacks.

One of the most significant innovations in the development of the naginata blade was the addition of a thick cross-section at the base of the blade, along with a series of ridges and grooves called *naginata-hi*. This thick cross-section allows the weapon to absorb considerable force at its base. Thus, impact against the legs and body of a horse, against armor, or even the ground in the event of a miss, would not result in the blade snapping off at the base. In addition, the blade and thus the entire weapon is balanced nearer to the middle, rather than out at the tip, making it easier to maneuver. The grooves and ridges lighten the blade somewhat, allowing for an even thicker cross-section without sacrificing any strength (each groove is one-half of a cylinder, the strongest three-dimensional shape. Energy would be transferred through the blade without any sheering force).

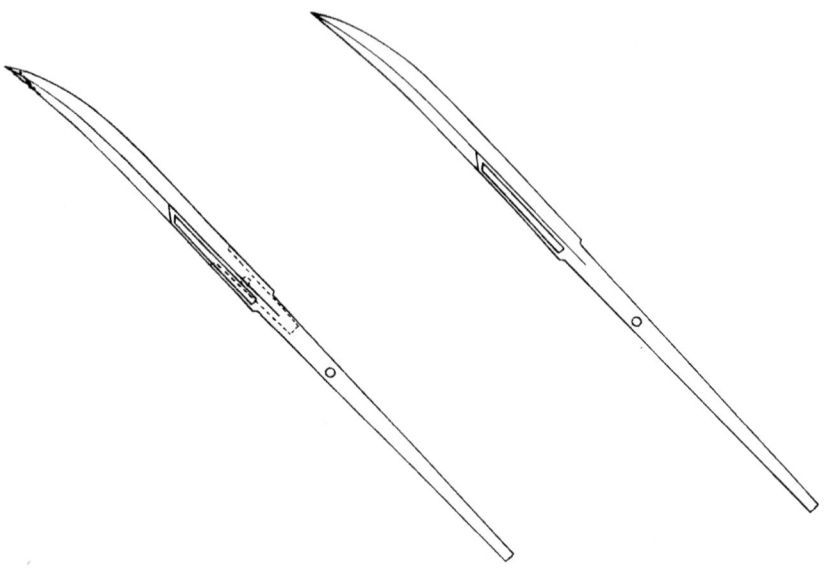

Left: Naginata naoshi. The dotted line indicates where the blade was cut and reworked to make it into a sword. Right: Typical early naginata blade with the ridgeline extending to the tip. *Sketches by Shinji Marumori.*

These first naginata were quite heavy weapons, used to cut the legs of horses and to crash through one's enemy's defenses: both their blocking weapon and their armor. They can also be used in thrusting attacks. Naginata remained in use throughout Japan's years of war from the Heian period all the way through to the Azuchi-Momoyama period (1568–1603 C.E.). They flourished, however, during the Nambokucho period (1333–1392 C.E.), when giant weapons were the rule and combat on foot, just coming into its own, relied on power as the epitome of the warrior's arsenal. Blades were often over a yard long. Naginata of this period featured blades that were more curved than earlier versions, and often the cutting edge flared out in a graceful sweep. Some time in the fourteenth or fifteenth century, these massive weapons came to be called *nagamaki*. This is a common name, but no one can say exactly what it means. *Nagamaki* literally means "long wrapping/turning." Some historians state that this refers to a form of wrapping around the shaft. Others claim it refers to the use of the weapon. *Nagamaki* are usually considered to be heavy, long-bladed, relatively short-shafted naginata. They can be rather awkward weapons, requiring a tremendous amount of strength to use. A fighter can be at a disadvantage if forced into a defensive attitude, particularly if his opponent is able to get inside the arc of the blade. But, used well, it is a terrifying weapon. It is swung in a seemingly unceasing, rolling attack, with cuts swooping in from all directions, and thrusts suddenly coming out of the windmill motions. The warlord Uesugi Kenshin is said to have had a special one-hundred soldier squad armed with *nagamaki*. There are only a few schools remaining in Japan which practice using weapons of this proportion and in this manner: the Araki-ryu, the Kashima Shinto-ryu and the Toda-ha Buko-ryu. Also notable is the Higo Ko-ryu (Amdur, 1994/95), which has created an extremely sophisticated method of wielding this seemingly awkwardly proportioned weapon.

Evidence in battle pictures and accounts indicates that different types of naginata were occasionally wielded on horseback, the *bushi* having trained to ride no-handed with bow and arrow. Due to its huge blade and great weight, the naginata would have been used like a scythe in a headlong charge into the enemy ranks. It would have been virtually unblockable. Once the initial momentum of the charge was lost and the warriors required maneuverability, they may have thrown aside their naginata and drawn their *tachi*. The *Kempo Ryaku Ki Fukugen* of Kubota Genseion states that "to use the nagamaki on horseback, you have to learn to wield it like a *tachi*. You must have immense power and absolute control of the stirrups, for, if not, it is easy to cut off your own horse's head."

At some time, smiths began to make their blades so that the ridgeline curved upwards to finish in the back edge of the blade, several inches behind the point (see illustration, p. 20). This was a brilliant innovation. The blade was still very heavy at the base, which, despite its length, made the naginata an extremely well-balanced weapon. But as can be seen, it was now also weighted at the tip. This helped the blade to cut extremely well. In addition, the thicker cross-section made it less likely to break off at the tip.

In the fifteenth century, more and more weapons featured the addition of a hand guard (*tsuba*) at the base of the blade. This served to deflect an enemy's blade from slipping up the shaft to cut off one's fingers. Given the weight and leverage of a naginata and the power of anyone who is strong enough to use it well, I can say from personal experience that it is quite difficult to neutralize that power and slide one's own weapon up toward the attacker's hands without exposing openings in one's own defenses. This is particularly true when using a sword.

That hand guards became almost "standard issue" by the sixteenth century indicates that the average sword and naginata fighter had become formidable indeed.

NAGAMAKI

Nagamaki by Kata Yama Ichimonji, thirteenth century, beginning of Kamakura Period. This enormous blade was made by a smith of Bizen, one of the great centers of swordmaking. The ridgeline ends several inches behind the tip, giving it strength and balance. The shaft is very simple without decorations. The blade has the graceful proportions that became common in the thirteenth and fourteenth centuries. *Courtesy of Otsuka Kogeisha.*

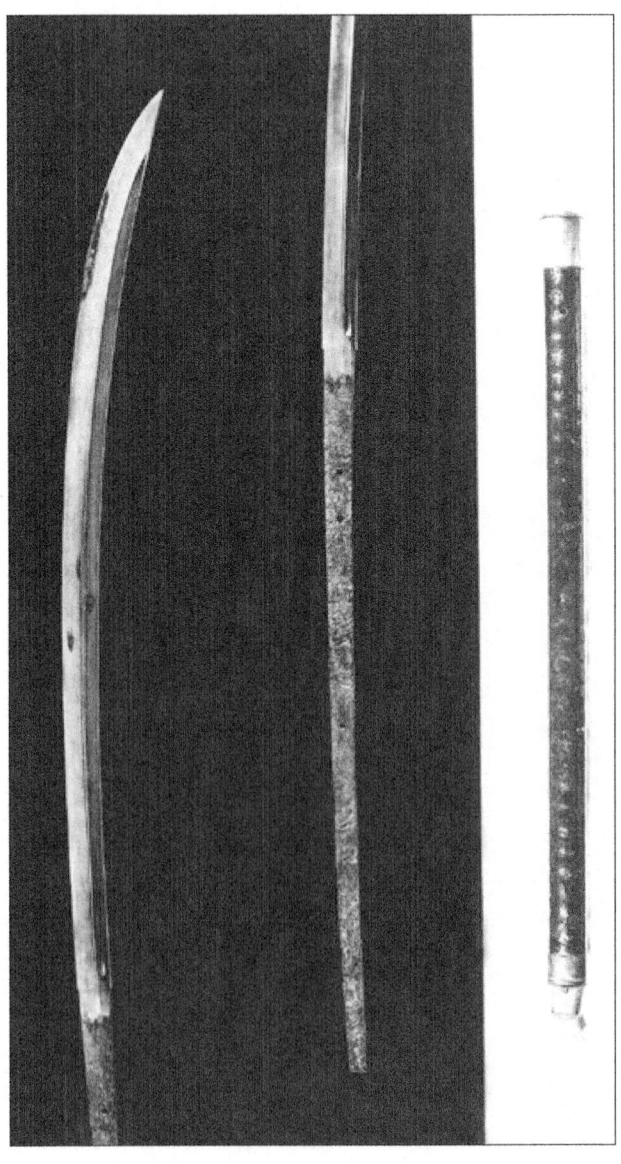

NAGINATA

Naginata by Bishi Osafune Jyu Kagemutsu. Early fourteenth century, at the end of the Kamakura Period. This long, slender blade with the ridgeline running to the tip is typical of many naginata in the Heian and Kamakura periods. *Courtesy of Otsuka Kogeisha.*

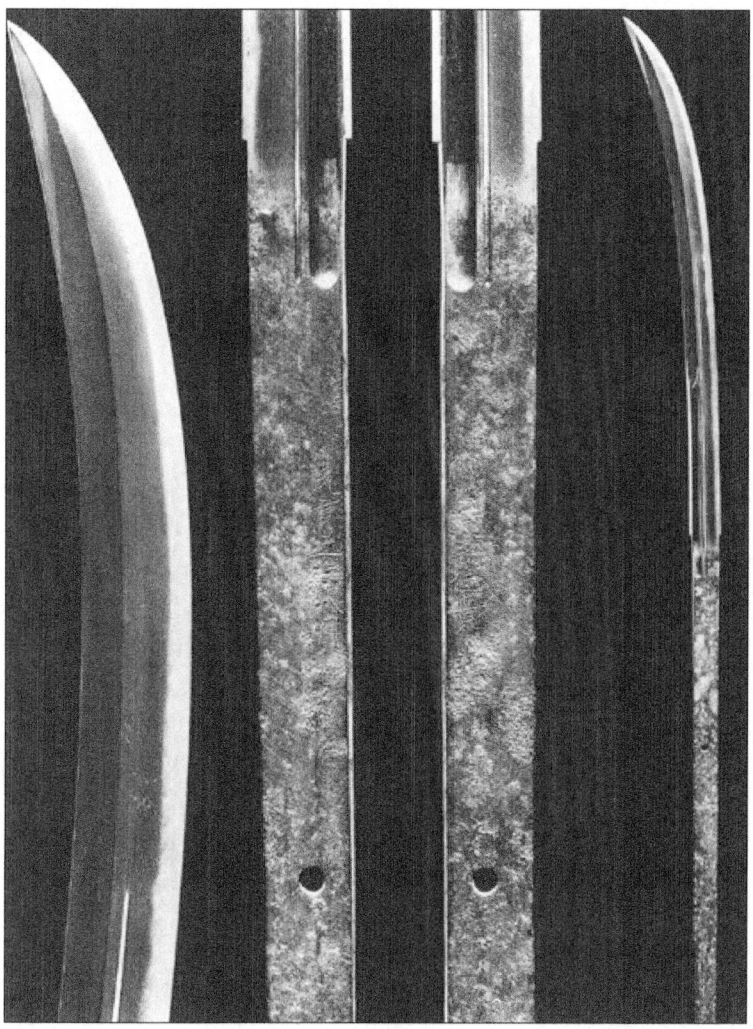

The blades of the fifteenth and sixteenth centuries generally became somewhat wider and shorter. They were extremely powerful, functional weapons but had lost some of the beautiful proportions of the earlier blades. As the blade was shortened, the shaft was lengthened and the weapon began to be used in a different manner. This long, heavy weapon is often referred to as *o-naginata* (great naginata).[3] It was probably at this time that different characters were used to write the word, changing *chotou* (long blade) to *naginata* (reaping blade).

This change in reading has two sources. First of all, extremely long swords came to be used in the thirteenth and fourteenth centuries. The names of these swords, called *choto*, were written with the same characters as the names of the early naginata, and it is likely that the characters were changed in part to avoid confusion. In addition, the weapon was now used in a different manner than a "long sword," and it was easy to envision it sweeping through opponents like a sickle through wheat.

The shafts of some naginata were elaborately and beautifully bound. They were presented as awards to warriors for exceptional deeds. Among these weapons were the *hirumaki naginata*, the shaft usually long and bound in rattan in various patterns; the *ao-gai hirumaki naginata*, the upper portion of the shaft inlaid with mother-of-pearl; and the *sendan maki naginata*, the "thousand-layer wrapping," which was bound in a pattern with fine hemp cord. One quarter inch of the shaft was bound and one eighth left unbound, this pattern continuing the length of the shaft. Then it was lacquered.

The *kagi naginata*, a final type, included an accessory more common to spears. This was an iron or bronze bar set perpendicular to the blade. It was used to deflect or even break an attacker's blade. This bar is known as the *hadome* (blade stopper) or *kagi* (hook, lock). If an enemy were to strike the *kagi* with the fine steel edge of his sword, it would bite into the relatively soft metal, and, with a quick twist, the holder of the *kagi naginata* could break or severely damage his opponent's weapon. As far as it is known, the only martial traditions that still practice with the *kagi naginata* is the Toda-ha Bukko-ryu and the Shin Gyo To-ryu.

The *o-naginata* came into wide distribution in the fifteenth and sixteenth centuries, and its use is exemplified in the Tenshin Shoden Katori Shinto-ryu (Amdur, 1994). In this marvelous tradition, the fighter holds the weapon in the middle and rapidly alternates cuts with the blade and blows with the *ishizuki*. The weapon is heavy enough that considerable cutting and striking force can be exerted. By holding the weapon in the middle, however, the warrior can use it almost as rapidly as a sword.

The sixteenth century Araki-ryu, on the other hand, is a school which prides itself on the strength of its practitioners and the almost extravagant violence of its techniques. This school also uses the *o-naginata* but, unlike the Katori Shinto-ryu, holds it at the end. With years of training, the practitioner is able to whirl the weapon at great speed. Postures are often low and crouching and footwork is quite fast. The weapon is swung with enormous power, with double or triple cuts to the same target, with sudden transitions into thrusts and slicing cuts to the neck, groin and armpits. The weapon is reversed and the butt end is used to finish off a downed opponent or crack across the temple in close quarters.

NAGAMAKI

Naginata by Koresuke of Bizen in the mid-fourteenth century. This heavy functional blade became an increasingly common style in the fifteenth and sixteenth centuries. *Courtesy of Otsuka Kogeisha.*

One martial tradition, which sadly is only maintained as a collateral practice by a few members of the Ono-ha Itto-ryu, brought the use of the long, heavy naginata to what are probably its limits. This is the Choku Gen-ryu. Founded by Kasai Denyemon Kanyu, this school originally featured sword versus sword, staff fighting and *jumonji yari* (spear with a cross piece) forms, but only the naginata versus sword forms have been preserved. There were two lines of this school until very recently. Shiradori Ichiko, a teacher of one line, is now deceased and she seems to have left no disciples. The other line was headed by

Sasamori Junzo, who was also a famous kendo instructor and the head of the Ono ha Itto-ryu. He died at the age of ninety about twenty years ago. According to an instructor with whom I conversed almost fifteen years ago, some of his students of the Ono Ha Itto-ryu occasionally practiced the forms of the Choku Gen-ryu. However, without a head instructor, they more or less consider this martial tradition finished as a "living" school. About twenty years ago, the national association of modern naginata (the Naginata Renmei) made a film of the remaining fifteen or so martial traditions that they could locate which practiced naginata. To my knowledge, there is only one copy of this film and, although poorly cared for, it was rather jealously guarded by the Naginata Renmei. Through the kindness of Higashi Tomoko, master instructor of the Jikishin Kage-ryu Naginata-do, I was lucky enough to be permitted to view it. Among the martial traditions shown was the Choku Gen-ryu. The description that follows is based on my viewing.

Choku Gen-ryu used two naginata, the larger of which was imposingly heavy and nine feet long. This was used in long looping cuts from feet to head, cutting the sword fighter's arms and trunk. In the forms, the sword does not threaten the naginata; it seems that the sword fighter is a moving practice dummy to help develop the naginata fighter's skills. The naginata is used to smash down the opponent's blade, to thrust, and to cut the wrists to fend off an attack to the head. Perhaps because of the length and weight of the weapon, it is not raised above the head for downward attacks. The essentials of Choku Gen-ryu seem to have required a constant sweeping back and forth in figure eights, from low to high and side to side.

Putting Aside the Naginata

The naginata first began to be supplanted after the Mongol invasions of 1274 and 1281. Japanese warriors were impressed with the Mongol's group tactics, particularly their use of the spear. It was obvious that five or ten closely-packed spearmen were more than a match for one or two fighters with naginata, who, due to the space required to use their weapons, could not concentrate in greater numbers. Smiths began to develop a tanged spear called *yari*. The use of the spear encouraged the development of sophisticated battlefield formations and strategies.

As time passed, armies of conscripts were drafted and sent to the field of battle in larger and larger numbers. This trend culminated in the Sengoku (1467 C.E.–1568 C.E.) and Azuchi-Momoyama periods with armies of the tens, even hundreds of thousands. Battlefield formation and siege tactics became far more important than individual valor, and first the spear and then the gun (introduced to Japan in 1543) became the weapons of choice. However, there were still those who fought with naginata, even up to the last days of war in medieval Japan.

One of the most famous was Anazawa Mondo no Tsuke Morihide, the founder of the Anazawa-ryu Naginatajutsu.

Anazawa had studied under the fifth headmaster of the Katori Shinto-ryu. In addition to Anazawa-ryu, he was claimed as the founder of Shinto-ryu Nagatachi (long sword) and Isshin-ryu Bojutsu (staff). He served the warlord Toyotomi Hideyori and often engaged in contests before him. Armed with a wooden naginata, he would fight two opponents armed with sharpened bamboo spears. He was never defeated in those matches. He died in the summer battle for Osaka castle in Hideyori's service in 1615, when the victor, Tokugawa Ieyasu, succeeded in uniting Japan as a single nation. It is illustrative of the degeneration of values at this time that the warrior who claimed to have defeated Anazawa in single combat was proven to have lied. He was really near defeat himself when a group of his retainers rescued him and killed Anazawa from behind.

The Anazawa-ryu is now, like so many other ryu, extinct. The twelfth-generation head instructor died at any early age and only a small portion of her teachings were passed down. Like Choku Gen-ryu, the only record we have of this tradition is a small portion on the film I mentioned above. What is preserved is not very inspiring, at least in contrast to what a fighter one imagines Anazawa must have been. The film presents two women wearing kimono without the customary *hakama* (pleated culottes) over it. The *hakama*, covering the legs, enables both men and women to practice without exposing their legs as they would with only kimono. Both women had to take small shuffling steps so that their kimono were not disarranged, offering, to this outsider at least, almost a parody of Japanese femininity. Their movements were so delicate and graceful, yet so bound by the artificial constraints of their clothing that their practice bore little resemblance to combative practice. The sword user did not attack the individual with the naginata, but merely cut through the air some distance away from her. The naginata was swept in broad movements with little power. The forms were all rather dramatic, at times resembling *kembu*, a style of dancing with weapons. I doubt that Anazawa would recognize these women as practicing anything like what he had created.

Naginata and Women

After 1600, most of the naginata blades were made for the training of *bushi* women. The subject of women and naginata is far too broad a topic to discuss in detail in this article. Briefly, though, women had used naginata from ancient days, though the extent of their training is unknown. It is known that women rarely went on the battlefield by choice or expectation, but in emergency situations the naginata was considered the weapon most appropriate to women's physique and to the circumstances in which they would fight. This would include fending off attackers on horseback and also men armed with a variety of weapons. Women were at a particular disadvantage at close range due to most men's skill at grappling (sumo was likely practiced by most Japanese males from the tenth century onward. Social constraints made practice by women very unlikely.). The naginata would enable a woman to make it quite costly for anyone trying to attack them. The other major weapon of women was the dagger (*kaiken*). Quite a few systems of training feature forms in which the attacker gets inside the arc of the naginata and the practitioner quickly throws it aside while drawing a dagger in the same motion. The attacker, suddenly much closer than he would wish to be, is stabbed.

Hojo Masako, the wife of Sengoku period daimyo Takeda Katsuyori (1546-1582) is depicted carrying a naginata during an attack. Her husband was defeated by Oda Nobunaga and had to flee, his wife going with him. However, Katsuyori was resigned to die and prompted her to leave. She refused and committed suicide with her husband.
Ⓢ *Print by Adachi Ginko (active c.1870–1908). Public domain.*

It may be objected that the war naginata must have been too heavy for most women to handle, but that is not so. *Bushi* women of these early years were no frail maidens, cloistered in rooms and delicate pursuits. They were frontiers women. They worked with their hands. They farmed, lifted and carried and were, on the average, likely to be far tougher than most men in twentieth century urban society.

At any rate, the imposition of the Tokugawa government in the early seventeenth century led to strict social controls on all strata of society. Such controls fell especially heavily upon women. The naginata became an emblem of a glorious past, of a life spent in self-sacrifice, much like the lives of male *bushi*, although the form of that sacrifice and the way it was played out in society was far different. The use of the naginata became more formalized and stylized in specific martial traditions which became associated with women. Movements became precise and quick, and the weapons themselves had small slender blades, not suitable for warfare, although still potent weapons for one-on-one combat against unarmored opponents.[4] They were hafted to light shafts and the *bushi* women practiced with them less for combat than to acquire the values and strengths considered appropriate for women of their class. They could certainly be used in single combat, but their sophisticated, elegant movements were far different from those used by early warriors and monks, charging on the field of battle in a melee of dust, screams and blood.

NOTES

[1] Researcher Larry Bieri (1982) points out, however, that they could have been remounted into the present light shafts at a later date. If there was a previous shaft, it could well have been much heavier.

[2] The *shang-dao* is known to have been incorporated into one system of Okinawan combat, the Ryuei-ryu, under the Japanese name of *bisento* (Skoss, 1994). As is well known, Chinese martial arts are the chief foreign influence on the fighting arts of Okinawa. However, Okinawa is likely to have had no influence upon Japanese warfare because Okinawa did not become part of Japan's sphere of influence until the sixteenth century.

[3] The word *ko-naginata* is also seen in some texts. In its earliest usage, it indicates a shorter version of the *o-naginata*, "ko" meaning small. However, it was still a stout, heavy weapon of approximately seven to seven-and-a-half feet in length. In later times, *ko-naginata* indicated the slender lighter weapons that women came to specialize in using.

[4] The reader is urged to consider a similar comparison between an AK-47 or M-16 automatic weapon, developed for use on the battlefield, and a .38 caliber revolver or semi-automatic handgun, quite adequate for self-defense purposes and, in many respects, far more suitable to such an end than a weapon of war.

BIBLIOGRAPHY
English Language Sources

Amdur, E. (1994). Divine transmission katori shinto-ryu. *Journal of Asian Martial Arts*, 3(2): 48–61.

Amdur, E. (1995). The rise of the curved blade. *Furyu*, 1(4): 58–68.

Amdur, E. (1994/95). Higo ko-ryu. *Furyu*, 1(3): 49–54.

Bieri, L. (1982). Naginata—The Japanese halberd. *Hoplos*: 4(1).

Compton, W. A., J. Homma, K. Sato, and M. Ogawa. (1982). *Nippon to—Art swords of Japan*. Tokyo: Japan House Gallery.

Draeger, D., and R. Smith. (1969). *Asian fighting arts*. Tokyo: Kodansha, Ltd.

Draeger, D. (1974). *The martial arts and ways of Japan, Volumes I-III*. New York: Weatherhill.

Draeger, D., and Warner, G. (1982). *Japanese swordsmanship*. New York: Weatherhill.

Knutsen, R. (1963). *Japanese polearms*. London: The Holland Press.

Mason, P. (1977). *A reconstruction of the hogen-heiji monogatari emaki*. New York: Garland Pub., Inc.

McCullough, H. Craig (Trans.). (1979). *Taiheiki*. Rutland: Charles E. Tuttle Co.

Ogasawara, N. (1970). *Japanese swords*. (D. Kenny, Trans.). Tokyo: Hoikusha.

Reischauer, E. (1947). *Chronological chart of far eastern history*. Cambridge: Harvard Press.

Sadler, A. (Trans.). (1941). *Heike Monogatari*. Tokyo: Kimiwada Shoten.

Skoss, M. (1994). Ryukyu Kobudo. *Aiki News*, 21(2): 14–15 and 27.

Wilson, W. (Trans.). (1971). *Hogen monogatari*. Tokyo: Sophia University Press.

Yamada, N. (1916). *Ghenko—The Mongol invasion of Japan*. New York: E. P. Dutton.

Japanese Language Sources

Imamura, Y. (1971). *Nihon Kengo Shi*. Tokyo: Shinjumbutsu Orai Sha. [Great swordmasters of Japan].

Ishioka, H. and K. Okada. (1978). *Hiroshi kato, Nihon no kobujutsu*. Tokyo: Shinjumbutsu Orai Sha. [Study of notable martial traditions].

Tokyo Kyoiku Daigaku, Taiikushi Kenkyusitu, Zen Nihon Budo Senshu. (1967). *Kobudo Shinkokai*. Tokyo: Jimbutsu Orai Sha. (Imamura Yoshio, Ed.). [Massive collection of articles and historical material pertaining to many old martial traditions].

Mitamura, K. (1939). *Dai Nippon naginata do kyoden*. Tokyo: Shubundo Shoten. [Prewar school instructor's book for Tendo-ryu].

Yazawa, I. (1916). *Naginata no hanashi*. [A small article by the naginata instructor of Japan Women's University].

chapter 3

The Warrior's Prayer: Tokugawa Yoshimune Revives the Yabusame Ceremony

by Reinier H. Hesselink, Ph.D.

Yabusame at Tsurugaoka Hachimangu Shrine, Kamakura.
Photos courtesy of the Japan National Tourist Organization.

In 1636 Hendrick Hagenaer, a Dutch trader, observed the following:

> On the 18th [of October] the archery festival was celebrated [at Hiradol in the following manner: in the wide street in front of the house of the highest official, a screen was erected as a target. The Japanese appeared on horseback, armed with bow and arrow, as if they were going to war. They spurred their horses, and when they had reached the target at a distance of about one and a half fathoms,[1] they released their arrows. When they hit the target, they were honored by the spectators with great acclamations. Each archer ran the track two or three times. It was strange and incomprehensible.
> – Hagenaer, 1646: 100

Today, Japan is one of the few places left in the world where the art of mounted archery is still practiced. This is all the more surprising when we remember that Japan has been an agricultural society for most of its history and that mounted archery, born among the nomads of Central Asia, is an imported art (Hesselink: 27-47). What is more, the military application of mounted archery has been obsolete since the introduction of firearms into Japan. Consequently, we see a rapid decline of the art from the second half of the sixteenth century onwards. During the seventeenth century, most of the places which had traditionally organized mounted archery ceremonies ceased to do so. The above-quoted Dutch account, therefore, must be an isolated example of a languishing art, possibly performed to impress the foreign $6 tourists." According to Japanese sources, by the early eighteenth century, the *yabusame* ceremony had ceased to be performed until the eighth Tokugawa shogun, Yoshimune, ordered it revived. Since that time, mounted archery has become an art which is alive for its own sake only. And it may be that we glimpse here at something quintessentially Japanese.

There are very few men today who practice the art, for the effort required and the costs are prohibitive while social payoffs are non-existent. There are, also, relatively few people in the world who have had the chance to observe it. Only those fortunate enough to have attended one of the rare occasions on which true yabusame is performed know something of the thrills of being a spectator and participant in this ceremony. But even more elusive is the deeper emotion of being an archer who has hit the three targets which are traditionally erected along the track. Mounted archery is the most exclusive of the martial arts.

Tokugawa Yoshimune is known for his wise management of the Ki domain he inherited, his love of learning and his patronization of the so called Kyoho reforms which sought to increase the tax base of the Bakufu (Tsuji, 1962). However, the most detailed information we have of this shogun's personal life concerns his love for horses and his insistence that all those in his closest environment share this hobby with him.[2] We can assume that, in 1684, the future shogun was born into a rustic and down-to-earth setting, for his mother seems to have been a peasant girl from the village of Kose who had caught the roving eye of the Dainagon, his father. At the time, nothing seemed more unlikely than this infant's succession to the shogunate, for Yoshimune was only the fourth son of Tokugawa Mitsusada, the representative of the House of Ki, while the son of Mitsusada's cousin Iemitsu, Tsunayoshi, had only been shogun for four years and Iemitsu's grandson Ienobu was already twelve years old.

In 1716, however, Ienobu's son Ietsugu died at the age of seven. Ietsugu had been shogun since he was three, after the death of his father in 1712. All of Yoshimune's own brothers had already passed away as well, and so the opportunity presented itself to Yoshimune to checkmate his rivals from Owari and Mito and to become the eighth Tokugawa shogun. After his move to Edo, Yoshimune quickly replaced most of the personal following of Ienobu with his own men and it was not long before evidence of his interest in horses appeared in a variety of source materials (Fukai: 399-433).

The Dutch representative, for example, on his second visit to Edo after Yoshimune's succession to the shogunate, was closely questioned about Dutch horses and the feasibility of importing large horses from Holland.[3] Previously, in the seventeenth century, Iemitsu and his son Ietsuna had also tried to improve Japan's breeding stock by importing horses from Holland, but the number of horses imported had been small (Iwao, 1980: 12-34). This time plans on a greater scale seemed to have been undertaken (Saito, 1922: 51-63). Orders went out to contact representatives of all four foreign countries with which Japan entertained regular relations.

The first to comply with the shogun's request were the Koreans, who brought two horses in 1719.[4] The Chinese followed the next year also with two horses. Even the Ryukyans brought specimens of their horses, for on April 8, 1725, the shogun is recorded to have viewed his retainers riding such horse.[5] The Dutch procrastinated until they were firmly ordered to supply horses of specific dimensions and had been assured that the volume of trade allowed would be increased by twenty-five percent to pay for this special request. Finally, the first Dutch horses arrived in the summer of 1725.

Yoshimune's concern with horses was not limited to improving the stock of the shogunal pastures. The methods of riding in the four foreign countries were compared to those in Japan, and the differences in horse gear and care were closely studied. A Chinese horse doctor[6] was brought to Nagasaki and with the Dutch horses of 1725 came a German riding instructor, Hans Jurgen Keyserling, who became a regular fixture of the Deshima crowd for the next ten years.[7] In 1729, when he was allowed to make his bed next to the shogunal stables at Obama (Hama rikyu), he became the first European to be lodged outside the usual inn for Dutchmen [the Nagasakiya] during their stay in Edo. At that time, he was asked a thousand and one questions on European horsemanship by an interpreter, Imamura Gen'emon, who later compiled the *Seisetsu hakuraku hikkei* or a *Manual of Western Style Horsekeeping* (Iwao, 1980: 89-189). Keyserling was so well liked by the horsemen around Yoshimune that he was asked to come back in 1735. The latter time he was ordered by his superiors in the Dutch East India Company to keep a detailed diary, which is now a good source for understanding the atmosphere around Yoshimune. The Japanese were especially eager to see Keyserling shoot his gun from horseback.[8] And on May 29, 1735, the German performed in front of the shogun:

> Arriving in the Castle at eight o'clock in the morning, I started riding around ten on a long track in His Majesty's and the crown prince's presence. After I had ridden three horses I had to come close to his Majesty, around twelve feet away from him, to a spot where a post had been erected. I was brought a horse which I was supposed to make walk around on the long leash. After I had done this, I was brought a saddled horse to ride. While Mr. Sanuemon stood next to the post telling me what to do, the shogun told Nagato no kami what he wanted to see. He also asked whether the horse understood the commands. Nagato no kami answered him yes, the horse understood my command.[9]

In contrast with the official treatment which the Dutch factors had grown used to, the Japanese were extremely eager to please Keyserling, whose great knowledge of horses was just as impressive to them as his simple and modest demeanor.

All of this concern with horses becomes fully comprehensible only in the light of a simultaneous research project commissioned by the shogun into the traditions of Japan's mounted archery ceremony known as yabusame. The etymology of this term is not clear, but the explanation most often given is that it is a contraction of yabasemuma, a compound meaning "arrow" and "galloping horse." The characters traditionally used to write the word are "flowing" (*nugarem*), "turnip-shaped arrow" (*kaburaya*) and "horse." On the start of Yoshimune's project the *Teijo zakki* states:

> The practice of yabusame had been discontinued since the time of the Muromachi shoguns . . . and during the Kyoho period when Lord Yutokuin[10] thought that yabusame should be revived, the details of the ceremony were not clear. Therefore, a request went out to the various houses and provinces to record the traditions from all directions and present them to the shogun. Urakami Yagozaemon was ordered to collect these writings, which were summarized in a book called *Yabusame ruiju*.[11]

Next, according to the *Tokugawa jikki*, on December 10, 1724, the inspector Ogasawara Heibei Tsuneharu was ordered to teach mounted archery to the shogun's close attendants.[12] We have to take this entry with a grain of salt, for the first time mounted archery was performed in front of the shogun himself occurred less than a year later, on November 30, 1725.[13] It is most unlikely that the archers involved had learned the art from scratch in the previous eleven months. Ten archers took part, all of them men who had come with the shogun to Edo from Ki ten years before. It is probable, therefore, that Yoshimune had been encouraging the practice of mounted archery since he became shogun and possibly even when he was still only daimyo of Ki.

All these men were employed as pages or chamberlains, the positions closest to the shogun inside Edo Castle, and they would constitute the inner core of Yoshimune's mounted archery force during the Kyoho period and beyond. Their average age upon this first recorded performance of mounted archery was, as far as I can determine,[14] thirty-four, another indication that whatever the truth of the perilous position of mounted archery at this time, these men at least had been practicing for longer than the one year the *Tokugawa jikki* ostensibly allows them. We will see below that the importance of praising the officially appointed teacher Ogasawara Heibei for his skills may have been a factor in this presentation of the facts.

The first among these mounted archers was Megata Morito, the same man who was called Nagato no kami by Keyserling. Morito is also mentioned in the biography of Ogasawara Mochihiro as one of the two students assigned to him to learn the archery ceremony in 1721. Others participating at this time included Urakami, the compiler of the *Yabusame ruiju*, and Toki Sabee, the younger brother of the man who, in Keyserling's diary, is called the shogun's favorite "minion."[15] From the proximity of these men to the shogun himself we can, again, gauge the strength of Yoshimune's interest in the project.

It is unclear to what extent mounted archery had disappeared in Japan and how it was reestablished. According to the *Tokugawa jikki*, it had disappeared completely and two Chinese mounted archers were invited to teach the art.[16]

Important, also, is the terminology employed to indicate mounted archery. When Ogasawara Heibei was commissioned to teach, the word *kisha*, written with the characters for "horsemanship" and "shooting," was used. The entry in the Kyoho nichiroku on the archery practice of the next year, however, employs the word yabusame. In this connection, the *Teijo zukki* has:

> What we now know as *kisha* was first started during the Kyoho period by Lord Yutokuin who commanded his retainers to shoot and came to watch them do it. Ogasawara Heibei was ordered to organize the ceremony and teach it to the various warriors. The ceremony resembled *yabusame* in that they dug a *sakuri* in which they made their horses gallop and shot arrows at targets consisting of thin boards wedged in between [bamboo post ends, *hasamimono*].

In 1728, a large-scale ceremony was held for the first time and forty-six archers participated. This time, although the men who had performed in 1725 also took part, the average age of the archers was only thirty-one and we see, therefore, that now mostly younger men were allowed to show their skills. The ceremony, upon this occasion, was recorded to have been *yabusame*[17] although the *Teijo zakki* calls it, puristically, *kisha hasamimono*, or "mounted archery of the wedged-in targets." And an appendix to the reign of Yoshimune in the *Tokugawa jikki* has: ". . . it is said that because the rules of the ceremony had not been transmitted as such, [Yoshimune] ordered it renamed as kisha hasamimono and not *yabusame*. This he did from extreme modesty."

By refusing to use the word yabusame, these writers, following the shogun's lead, indicated their awareness that the ceremony had been recreated and did not qualify as "genuine" yabusame. They adduced other differences as well:

> In the ancient way of practicing yabusame. . . all the archers would shoot standing up in the saddle without shouting and anyone could wear the *mukabaki* without shogunal permission, and the place to aim for was not limited to the lower part of the target but any place the archer fancied. Only when the drawing of the bow had been delayed a bit, would the archers aim for the lower part.[18]

But most men were not historians of the martial arts, and so the term yabusame stuck among the record keepers of the Castle. From 1725 onwards, we find that the shogun viewed kisha two or three times a year, while yabusame was rare, being performed only twice during Yoshimune's shogunate, in 1728 and 1738. The *Tokugawa jikki* often omits the times the shogun viewed kisha but is relatively detailed about the occasions on which yabusame was performed.

The difference between the two types of mounted archery lies in the supreme presence during the ceremony. In the case of kisha, as we have seen, the supreme presence was the shogun himself. When yabusame was performed, however, the shogun would not be present in person but be represented by one of his gosoku. The supreme presence in the case of yabusame, then, was the divinity of the shrine where the ceremony was held. It follows that we can only speak of yabusame when mounted archery is performed at a shrine. During Yoshimune's reign, the shrine designated for the purpose was the Anahachiman Shrine, near Takadanobaba, a modern place-name, which, incidentally, derives from the Takada track associated with this shrine.

The appendix to the record of Ieharu's reign in the *Tokuguwa jikki* quotes Yoshimune's own words on why he revived yabusame: "Because I regretted that the ancient ceremony of mounted archery had died out and also because I wanted to test my retainers whether they were diligent or lazy, I usually went to view [mounted archery] of my own free will."[19] The term used here for mounted archery is *kyuba* (lit. "bow and horse"), which clearly means kisha and yabusame. As we can see, Yoshimune's ostensible motives in reviving the mounted archery ceremony were his regret at its disappearance and the opportunity it provided him to judge the qualities of his men.

If we first take up the latter point, we are justified in asking how far prowess in mounted archery influenced the careers of the men involved. I have identified sixty-seven mounted archers among Yoshimune's retainers. Twenty-three of them, or more than a third, started their careers in the *koshogumi*, the guards protecting the shogun's pages. There were also nine *kosho* or pages, a post reserved for boys of prominent bushi families and a springboard for an illustrious career in the shogunal bureaucracy. Eight of the mounted archers were *konando* or chamberlains, close attendants of the shogun and of a more advanced age than the pages. The rest of the men came from other units of the castle guards than the *koshogumi*: the *shoinban* (18) and the *oban* (9). Looking at the careers these men made, I found that, although their ability in mounted archery may have played a role in their initial posting, it did not seem to have influenced their subsequent careers. One archer, thirty-four-year-old Komai Toshimasa, was even promoted to chamberlain only five months after he had missed all his targets during the yabusame ceremony at the Anahachiman Shrine of 1728, There can be no doubt, however, that prowess in mounted archery bestowed status, if not power, in the form of gifts of gold and seasonal clothing from the shogun himself. The biographies of twenty-nine of these archers mention such highly valued gifts.

Photo courtesy of the Japan National Tourist Organization.

From the above it should be clear that with so many different influences converging at the time of Yoshimune's revival of yabusame, it is difficult to assess the role of the Ogasawara family in this process. The matter is further complicated because representatives from three different branches of the family seem to have been involved. The most senior of these was Ogasawara Heibei Tsuneharu (1666-1747),[20] who, by virtue of his age and high position as one of the shogun's inspector (*metsuke*), took precedence over Ogasaara Nui dono Mochihiro (1685-1759) although the latter came from a more senior branch of the family and had, upon Yoshimune's accession, been ordered to compile a written record of his family tradition.[21] The third Ogasawara to be involved in the yabusame revival was Iwami no kami Masanari, who had been a retainer of Yoshimune in Ki and had come to Edo as the shogun's gosoku.[22] We see him officiate as the shogun's representative on the occasions that yabusame was performed.

Although the Ogasawara are faithfully mentioned in the *Tokugawa jikki* as teachers of kisha and yabusame, they are most often recorded as recipients of tokens of the shogun's gratitude. They clearly did not have exclusive control over the form, content, place and timing of the ceremony. Moreover, according to the *Teijo zakki*, after the death of Ogasawara Heibei, it was not his son, the accomplished mounted archer Magoshichiro, but Nui dono Mochihiro who succeeded him. Thus, the general supervision over the shogun's mounted archers reverted to the more senior branch of the family.

I cannot escape the impression that the Ogasawara contribution at this time was of an especially ornamental kind and not so much in formal training. The fact that, as noted above, the first demonstration of mounted archery by the shogun's retainers from Ki was dated a mere eleven months after Tsuneharu's appointment, clearly points in this direction. The association with the Ogasawara family was, of course, of the utmost importance if the Kyoho reconstruction of yabusame was to have any claim to legitimacy at all, for the Ogasawara had been models for mounted archery from the mid-fifteenth century onwards when they became the teachers of the Ashikaga shoguns (Futaki, 1969: 29-60).

The Ogasawara influence in Yoshimune's time was greatest on matters of dress, order of precedence, and the behavior of the archers' companions. Everything up to the smallest detail of the archer's outfit had its significance although the meanings of many details have today been lost or are only known to those sharing in the secret oral traditions. The *Ogasawara-ryu kyuba hisho* or *Secret Book of Mounted Archery of the Ogasawara School*, for example, constantly refers to the oral teachings (*kuden*) and gives very little concrete information.[23]

Great efforts were made during the Edo period to leave nothing to chance. Traditionally, each archer was accompanied by a *kaizoe*, or someone to replace him if he became ill or was thrown off his horse. A *yumi-bukurozashi* carried an extra bow. Although he shot only three arrows, the archer would carry six. There were men to set up his targets, the *matodachi*, and others to pick up his arrows, the *yagari*. In our more secular age, fear of the consequences of failure has diminished and the concern with expense has increased. Gone are the sixteen men surrounding each archer on his way to the track and accompanying him on foot, and a referee decides nowadays if an archer whose horse has stumbled can make the run again (Saito, 1962: 32).

However, the concern with failure, as shown in the countless measures taken to prevent it, also points to a deeper reason for the ceremony to be performed: Yabusame revived many of the ancient magical practices in which mounted archery had played a role since the Nara period. Here I can only give a few examples. The skill involved in hitting the target was thought to be "a divine art which drives away evil spirits and cleanses all pollution."[24] It was the archer's duty to prepare himself by abstention for as long as seventeen days before the event. His targets were known as the "godhead" (*shinto*) and missed targets were not reused but broken in two by those in charge of picking up the pieces of the targets that had been hit.

The track proper or *sakuri* was dug between two low earthen mounds, called male and female, so that the archer and his horse danced, as it were, on a cord connecting yin and yang. The left side where the targets stood was the yang or male side of the track, and the symbolism of the arrows flying on this side is hard to misunderstand. Also, while galloping along the track, at one with the divinity, the archer would chant "in-yo, in-yo" in between each of the targets. Important in the yin-yang symbolism are the sexual undertones. The energy freed or evoked by the ceremony was thought to be ready for use for specific purposes. In 1728, the purpose was to cure the future shogun Ieshige of some sort of skin disease which had started on April 8th and had been treated with a washing of sake and water twelve days later. Yabusame was performed on April 23rd and a week later the future shogun seems to have been cured. The next day, noh was performed in gratitude over his recovery.[25] In 1738, the birth of Ieharu was celebrated and the ceremony was supposed to store energy for use by the future shogun.

It goes without saying that this belief in magic was a major component in Yoshimune's decision to revive the yabusame ceremony and it may constitute a large part of the reason why he regretted its disappearance. It is also clear that the countless precautions taken to prevent failure were in large part due to the uncertainty of the result of such tampering with the divine. To the men involved, it must have been as if they had used a recipe for a magic broth from an old book and they were unsure what demons it might call up. Happily, the outcome of the first occasion had been the cure of the later shogun Ieshige. Great must have been the relief among the shogun's men when the ceremony turned out as they had hoped.

Photo courtesy of the Japan National Tourist Organization.

"Strange and incomprehensible," was Hagenaer's comment on what he saw in Hirado. Now that we have analyzed the ceremony's meaning, a Japanese description should be less so:

The last archer was Miura Gorozaburo. He fitted a turnip head arrow to his *shirogefuji* bow, and calling out in a loud voice ["in-yo"], rode out to break the first target. Notching the second arrow to his bow, he raised his riding whip and spurred his horse. Hitting his second target, he again called out ["in-yo"] and raised his whip like before. Finally hitting his third target he reached the place to dismount from his horse and there he performed the act of *shaben* (discarding his whip).[26]

NOTES

[1] One and a half fathoms equals 2.74 meters.
[2] A hagiographic account of Yoshimune's love for and ability with horses can be found in the *Tokugawa jikki*, Yutokuin Gojikki furoku 12.
[3] *Daghregister.* (1718, March 28 and 30, April 5).
[4] *Tokugawa jikki*, Kyoho 4th year, 10th month, 1st day.
[5] Cf. MS copy at the Historiographical Institute of the University of Tokyo (hereafter abbreviated SHJ) *Kyoho nichiroku*, 10th year, 2nd month, 25th day.
[6] Called Liu Jingxian.
[7] According to the *Getsudokenmonshu*, Keyserling was thirty years old in 1726. SHJ MS copy Kyoho 11th year, 2nd month, 10th day.
[8] *Daghregister.* (1735, May 12).
[9] *Daghregister.* (1735, May 29). Cf. also *Tokugawa jikki*, Kyoho 20th year, 4th month, 8th day, and *Kyoho nichiroku* and *Okachikata munnenki*, same date.
[10] I.e. Tokugawa Yoshimune.
[11] Compilation started by Ise Teijo in 1763 and completed by his grandson Ise Teiyu in 1833, preserved at the Naikaku Bunko. Here translated from *Kojiruien*, vol. 44, p. 485.
[12] *Tokugawa jikki*, Kyoho 9th year, 10th month, 25th day.
[13] SHJ MS copy *Kyoho nichiroku*, 10th year, 10th month, 26th day.
[14] Using the biographies in the *Kansei choshu shokafu*, hereafter abbreviated KCSF.
[15] *Daghregister.* (1735, July 5).
[16] Yutokuin gojikki furoku 12.
[17] *Kyoho nichiroku*, 13th year, 3rd month, 15th day.
[18] *Teijo zakki*, loc. cit.
[19] *Kojiruien*, vol. 44, p. 487.
[20] KCSF, vol. 4, p. 17.
[21] KCSF, vol. 4, p. 12.

[22] KCSF, vol. 19, p. 60.
[23] SHJ MS copy.
[24] Cf. Mikikigusa, in: *Kojiruien*, vol. 44. p. 5 10.
[25] *Kyoho nichiroku*, 13th year, 2nd month, 29th day, 3rd month 12th, 15th, 22nd, and 23rd day.
[26] *Shogun Tokugawa reitenroku*, no. 4. Translated from *Kojiruien*, vol. 44.

BIBLIOGRAPHY

Daghregister. (1718, March 28 and 30, April 5).

Daghregister. (1735, May 12).

Daghregister. (1735, May 29).

Daghregister. (1735, July 5).

Fukai, M. (1977). "Kishu hanshi no bakushinka to kyoho kaikaku." *Tokugawa rinseishi kenkyusho kenkyukiyo*: 399-433.

Futaki, K. (1969). "Muromachi bakufu kyuba kojitsuke Ogasawara uji no seiritsu." *Kokugakuin Daigaku Nihon Bunka Kenkyujo Kiyo*, 24: 29-60.

Hagenaer, H., (1646). "Scheep-vaart naer de Oost-Indien" in *Begin ende woortgang wande wereenigde Neederlandtsche Oost-Indische Campagnie* vol. 4. Amsterdam: Commelin.

Hesselink, R. (1991). "The introduction of the art of mounted archery into Japan." *Transactions of the Asiatic Society of Japan*, 4th series, vol. 6: 27-47.

Iwao, S. (1980). *Meiji izen yoma no yunyu to xoshoku*. Tokyo: Nichiran Gakkai.

Saito, A. (1922). "Tokugawa Yoshimune no yoma yunyu to waran bajutsushi no torai" *Shigaku Zasshi*, vol. 33, 12: 51-63.

Saito , N. (1962). *Yabusame hongi*. Nikko: Toshogu.

Tsuji, Z. (1962). *Tokugawa Yoshimune koden*. Nikko: Toshogu.

chapter 4

Hikiotoshi Uchi Kihon: Jodo's Pull and Drop Strike

by Rick Polland, B.A.

Author practicing jodo at the Kashima Shrine, Ibaraki Prefecture.
The Shinto shrine is dedicated to the war god Takemikazuchi-no-mikoto.
All photographs courtesy of Rick Polland.

Introduction

Shindo Muso-ryu Jodo can be literally translated as the "Way to the Gods, Muso's Stick Way." This translation can be augmented with the additional note that the "way" came in a dream leading to an enlightened state (*satori*) for the ryu's founder, Muso Gonnosuke. Jodo, with an estimated 15,000 practicing adherents worldwide,[1] has always remained in the shadows of the more well known kendo and iaido, arts that it predates by centuries. Jodo still retains its complex school of stick fighting and also incorporates Kasumi Shinto-ryu Kenjutsu (sword),[2] Ikkaku-ryu Juttejutsu (*jutte* or *sai*), Ittatsu-ryu Hojojutsu (tying up), Isshin-ryu Kusarigamajutsu (chain and sickle), and Uchida-ryu Tanjojutsu (*sutekijutsu*) into its curriculum.

Like other martial arts, jodo was taught to small groups of students. The late headmaster Shimizu Takaji (b. Dec. 31, 1896–d. June 22, 1978) looked to expand jodo through the Nihon Jodo Renmei (Japan Jodo Association) in 1955.[3] Shimizu and fourteen members met and decided to open jodo up to the world and efforts were made to popularize the art.[4] This was partially done so that this classical tradition would not slip into history. *Kihon*, or fundamental component parts, were first introduced by Shimizu about 1930[5] and would take on great importance in the development of a practical teaching method. The observance of kihon would enable consistent transmission to both satellite schools and larger numbers of students. Today, every jodo session begins with the twelve kihon. These exercises are not only a prelude to rigorous jo training but also serve as warm-up exercises. Kihon can be practiced as a solo exercise called *tandoku renshu*, or in pairs called *sotai renshu* with one person with a jo (*shidachi*) and another with a wooden sword (*uchidachi*).

TECHNICAL SECTION

This chapter will focus on the third of the twelve kihon: *Hikiotoshi Uchi* (pull and drop strike) in a solo exercise. It is interesting to note that there are minor adjustments that take place as the kihon are performed as when either paired with an opponent or as they are found in a solo kata. This kihon was selected out of sequence for several reasons:

1) For the beginning student, this kihon can be frustrating. In attempting to "master" Hikiotoshi Uchi, the student creates many short-term solutions that must actually be overcome and dismantled in the process of learning the technique. There is much to be learned from the errors associated with attempting this kihon, errors that shed light on the challenges of learning jodo in general.

2) This kihon recurs quite often in jodo within kata. The technique is one of the most powerful tools within the jodo arsenal when applied correctly.

3) It is said that when Shimizu was asked which concept in jodo was most challenging, he replied that he still didn't fully understand Hikiotoshi Uchi.

引落打	仕杖	打太刀
Hikiotoshi Uchi	Shidachi	Uchidachi
（ひきおとしうち）	（しだち）	（うちだち）
Pull and Drop Strike	Stick [side]	Wooden Sword [side]

When jo is paired against sword, Hikiotoshi Uchi is used to threaten the swordsman's head from the right or left. The jo should take the centerline, striking about three inches down from the tip of the sword (*monouchi*). The strike is a gliding motion as the jo continues forward. The strike directs the sword down and away while forcing the swordsman back. The top of the swordsman's head (*uto* point) is threatened throughout the action.

Hikiotoshi Uchi Ni Kamae
(The voice command given to start this kihon)

The kihon starts from an initial engagement posture (*tsune ni kamae*) (fig. 1). The student holds the jo in the right hand as the arm drops and rests naturally at the side of the body. The *joseki* (tip of the jo) is aimed at the center of the opponent (*suigetsu*) as the stick is gripped at center so that the jo balances in the hand. When one practices alone, he should imagine an opponent the same size as himself.

The student then moves the left foot forward into a "half-facing" position (*hanmi*) while simultaneously grasping the top end of the jo with the left hand. The fingers are splayed slightly and raised upward with the palm out from the chest as the jo comes to rest. The hand touches the left breast. The right hand rotates slightly as it slides down the jo. The arm remains extended with a slight elbow bend. The fingers of the right hand close lightly around the jo, with the thumb facing away from the body (fig. 2).

Students new to jo have a tendency to either drop their forward hand or let it drift out and away from the body while also pulling or wrapping the jo behind the back leg. These are bad habits that change the trajectory of the strike, making the successful execution of the kihon less likely (fig. 3).

In the guard posture, the rear foot is angled slightly more open than ninety degrees from the center line, but pivots forward to a sixty-degree angle as the stick starts to move. Beginners often drag their rear foot like an anchor, failing to put the foot in the right position. Another common mistake is to have both feet facing forward in too narrow a stance. Doing the kihon with this weakened platform takes the student off balance.

A stance that is too narrow does not allow the hips to rotate and travel through the strike. This can create a bouncing movement and result in changing the trajectory of the strike.

In kihon the movement of the joseki stops at eye level. In *sotai renshu* this movement would spiral down to about the level of the opponent's knee and then follow the centerline back up to the eyes. It is important to keep proper combative distance (*maai*) the entire time (fig. 4).

Hikiotoshi Uchi Hajime
(Command to begin the kihon)

The back arm lifts close to the body in a big circle (fig. 5). Toward the top of the arc, the back arm's range of motion becomes limited, forcing the forward arm to lift slightly and travel forward toward the tip of the sword. The front hand closes into a fist. This is done simultaneously with the right hip and leg rotating forward. The back leg continues traveling forward and stops as the jo concludes its forward motion. The jo should keep a forward pressure pushing the swordsman back (fig. 6–9).

If the hips rotate too soon or too late, the body is twisted and/or overextended, changing the angle of attack of the weapon. Often a beginning student, bringing too much forearm power to bear, while using imperfect form, will miss striking the sword and twist around like a pretzel, leaving the swordsman menacingly unaffected. A common mistake is to put too much speed and power in the back arm which mostly guides the jo. The back swing should remain slow, letting the forward arm gather speed while letting the body apply the force of the strike by sinking the hips on impact. The back hand pushes while the front hand pulls the jo into the strike. Let the jo fully extend and drop naturally in order to make a big motion.

A useful image in understanding the movement of the arms is that of an old train engine's wheels which moved locked in relation to each other by a steel rod.

The back hand pulls the jo back as the body returns to a "half-facing" position (*hanmi*) on the opposite side. The forward hand follows and pushes the jo back. The lead hand reverses grip by flipping over while the practitioner resets his position to begin another cycle. (Fig. 10-12 show left side movements and fig. 13-15 show the grip exchange).

Yame Motoe
(Voice Command to Stop)

Upon completion of a series of kihon, the student returns to the engagement stance in mental and physical preparation for the next kihon (fig. 16-17). Beginners often rush and blend the individual movements of the kihon and should be cautioned to do each individual step of the kihon. Upon gaining mastery, the student's form will become one fluid motion.

The creative artifices with which we try to figure out the movements of jodo are quite revealing. Jodo is an art that utilizes finesse as well as speed and power. Jodo has little tolerance for even the slightest changes in body mechanics. Some changes might reveal an opening, exposing the student to attack or even render a technique useless.

The beginner often tries to make the technique work by increasing forearm power and speed before getting the proper form and timing. The stick has a nasty way of humbling even the strongest and fastest of us who do not fully understand the mechanics of the movement. Once the movement is understood, the temptation remains to answer each new technique introduced, with speed and power. The stick serves as a great weapon of humility ensuring that the student remains baffled until he is able to let go of the worldly desire to smash the daylights out of an opponent.

This chapter is dedicated to the memory of Shimizu Takaji on the anniversary of his passing away on June 22, 1978. I am delighted to have had the privilege to train at the original Rembukan under his guidance. – R. Polland

ACKNOWLEDGEMENT

I would like to thank all of the members of the Rembukan Dojo for their assistance in the development of this chapter and especially to Mr. Thomas Calabrese, for his excellent photography skills, and Messrs. Anthony Woodward, Richard Strausbaugh, and Dan Pearson for their technical input. Through-out the course of writing this article, each assisted by being *uchidachi*. Mr. Richard Strausbaugh is seen with the author in the photos in this chapter. Any errors in this chapter are purely my own and due to my limited understanding of this most wonderful art.

NOTES

[1] Kaminoda Tsunemori. Interviewed by the author, (Kashima Jinja), September, 1996.
[2] Kaminoda Tsunemori. Interviewed by the author, (Annapolis, Maryland, and the Japanese Cultural and Information Center, Washington D.C.) October, 1996.
[3] The name was changed to *Zen Nihon Jodo Renmei* (All-Japan Jodo Association) in 1956. Matsui, K. (1993). The history of Shindo Muso-ryu Jojutsu. *International Hoplology Society*, p. 27.
[4] Kaminoda, Tsunemori. Interviewed by the author, (Zoshukan Temple, Tokyo), July, 1993.
[5] Matsui, K. (1993). The history of Shindo Muso-ryu Jojutsu. *International Hoplology Society*, p. Chronology.
[6] Jodo Kihon, *Martial Arts International*, Vol. 1/ No. 2 (March 1974), p. 18.

chapter 5

My Heart is the Target: An Interview with Archer Shibata Kanjuro

by Deborah Klens-Bigman, Ph.D.

All photos courtesy of D. Klens-Bigman.

Introduction

It is a hot, humid Sunday morning on Labor Day weekend of 1998. I stand about six feet away from a cloth-wrapped bale of straw set on a stand so its center is nearly at eye level. In my left hand, I hold a seven-foot traditional Japanese long bow. In my right, I have two unfletched aluminum arrows.

Breathing deeply and slowly, I perform the movements of the "seven coordinations", the first exercise in learning archery (*kyudo*) of the Heki Bishu Chikurin School.[1] First, I take a preliminary "ready" stance and position the bow. Then, the "coordinations": setting the feet, setting the body and nocking the arrow shaft, orienting the bow towards the target, raising the bow, and the draw. I pause at the greatest extent of the draw. Finally, I let go and release the arrow. The arrow buries itself in the straw bale. I hold for a moment of *zanshin* (with mind and body totally focused). Then, I bring the bow back to the starting position. I had accomplished what I trained for all weekend: my first shot.

As a meditative experience, the "first shot workshop" I undertook, sponsored by Miyako Kyudojo of Washington, D.C., was as good as it gets.[2] I was one of about 20 beginners who braved the incredibly hot holiday weekend for Friday night orientation, training in the "seven coordinations" all-day on Saturday and Sunday, when I took my first shot, and with subsequent practice on Monday. The event was held at Adelphi Manor Archery, a public archery range near Silver Springs, Maryland. The experience was relaxing, even invigorating after the successful completion of my first shot. Ultimately, however, exhilaration gave way to frustration as I failed to sink a shaft into the straw bale for the rest of the day (a common occurrence, I'm told). The weekend was supervised by instructors from Miyako, the Tokokyudojo of New York City, and other instructors from around the East Coast, all under the watchful eye of Shibata Kanjuro, 20th headmaster of the Heki Bishu Chikurin lineage. Miyako Kyudojo insisted on my participation in the workshop as a prerequisite for interviewing Mr. Shibata about his kyudo style as it has been practiced in the West for the past 18 years.

Background

Kyudo shares with other styles of archery the legacy of what is ostensibly the world's oldest stored energy weapon. Archeological evidence to support archery goes back at least 10,000 years. Bows and arrows were used for both hunting and warfare (Stein, 1988: 3).

Prototypes of the Japanese bow, a recurved composite (laminated) bow date back to the Jomon culture (c.10,000–250 B.C.E.) (Stein, 1998: 8). Though there is evidence of shorter bows in use, the longer bow has been favored for at least 1000 years (Hurst, 1998: 104). The long bow also developed its characteristic asymmetrical shape, with the grip below the mid-point.

Japanese bows have long had a religious or shamanic function. The twanging of a bowstring brought good luck to the birth of a child, or could send a Shinto priestess into trance.[3] By the Heian period (794–1192 C.E.), nobles used the bow for ceremonial purposes, for hunting, and for target shooting. *Bushi*, warriors whose primary job at this time was to defend and protect the nobles, were enlisted as both hunters and target-shooting contestants. By the time of the Kamakura Bakufu (1185–1333), bushi were holding their own hunts and contests (Onuma et al., 1993: 4; Hurst, 1998: 107–111).

The introduction of guns to Japan in 1543 forced a change in thinking about the deployment of men and weapons (Onuma et al., 1993: 17–18). The "way of the bow and horse" began evolving into a sport, while also retaining its spiritual and ritual functions (Stein, 1988: 12; Hurst, 1998: 38). Combat archery virtually ceased, for all intents and purposes, by the time of the Tokugawa shogunate, though bow techniques continued to be pursued as a skill by nobles and members of the samurai class. Shooting contests became popular, with contestants competing in age and distance categories. Records were set and broken. Prizes were awarded, and wagers were often laid on the outcome of a contest. At the same time, the Shinto and spiritual aspects of archery survived and became, at various times, affiliated with Buddhism and Zen. Some styles pursued both spiritual values and competition, while other styles favored one over the other (Hurst, 1998: 123, 140; Onuma et al. 1993: 18–19). It is important to note that sportive and spiritual aspects of practice were not considered to be mutually exclusive.

With the change of government in 1868, traditional martial arts became more accessible to the general public. Cameron Hurst notes all forms of martial arts declined in the beginning of the Meiji era as it repositioned itself from skills restricted to particular classes (nobles and samurai), to a broader appeal as a hobby to the civilian middle class and members of the new, Western-style military (1998: 170). However, while swordsmanship survived and kendo as the sportified form of sword practice became popular, kyudo struggled. Eventually, a few styles of kyudo survived, the largest three being the Heki School, the Honda School, and the ceremonial style of the Ogasawara School. At the beginning of the 20th century, teachers pushed to have kyudo made part of the secondary school curriculum, and they achieved some success when it was incorporated as an elective in the 1930's (Hurst, 1998: 171).

With the end of the Pacific War and the beginning of the Occupation, the Supreme Commander of the Allied Powers (SCAP) banned kyudo along with other Japanese martial arts. However, kyudo's long association with sport rather than militarism held it in good stead. Kyudo practice was allowed to resume before other budo, and the Zen Nihon Kyudo Renmei (ZNKR) was formed in 1949, with the first official tournaments held the following year, well before the end of the Allied Occupation in 1952 (Hurst, 1998: 173).

Overlooking a practice field, Shibata Kanjuro shares his views on kyudo with Dr. Klens-Bigman.

ZNKR teaches a standard style of shooting which many kyudo groups now practice along with their more traditional styles.[4] ZNKR also follows the low to high grade (*kyu-dan*) ranking system originated by judo founder Kano Jigoro, adapted for kyudo in the 1920's and now common to other contemporary budo (Hurst, 1998: 171). Recently, kyudo has enjoyed a resurgence as a competitive sport among Japanese high school and college students. Since the beginning of the 20th century, kyudo has been promoted as an ideal sport for women. As a result, many present-day students and teachers are female. New Year's broadcasts on Japanese television often include a long line of young women, dressed in spectacular long sleeve kimono, taking their "first shot" of the New Year.

Shibata Kanjuro, in addition to being headmaster of the Heki School's Bishu Chikurin branch, is also hereditary bowmaker to the Imperial House of Japan. He inherited the title and bowmaking skills through the *iemoto* tradition, wherein one person of a generation is chosen as a successor. Mr. Shibata has made both ceremonial bow and more practical bow for kyudo practice.

Almost 20 years ago, Mr. Shibata met a student of Chogyam Trungpa

Rinpoche[5] (1939–1987), an adept of the Kagyu lineage of Tibetan Buddhism. Chogyam Trungpa created a form of spiritual training known as Shambhala, popularly referred to by students as "the way of the warrior" (Shambhala Centre 2000, n.p.). Chogyam Trungpa invited Mr. Shibata to teach his style of kyudo to the Shambhala students as a meditative practice. Mr. Shibata took up residence in Colorado and introduced his style of kyudo to the meditation students. Soon Shambhala adherents from Colorado to the East and West Coasts and parts of Canada and Europe were practicing kyudo of the Heki Bishu Chikurin School.[6]

Though Chogyam Trungpa died in 1987, Mr. Shibata continues to teach Shambhala adherents and other interested students. These days, he divides his time between his family home and workshop in Kyoto, Japan and the West. His base in the United States is in Boulder, Colorado, from which he travels in late spring, summer and early fall throughout the United States, Canada and Europe, supervising intensive kyudo practice at a number of venues, including the Tibetan Buddhist monastery in Vermont, Karme Choling, founded by Chogyam Trungpa, and the Zen Mountain Monastery in Woodstock, New York. Unlike most contemporary budo teachers, Mr. Shibata uses a *menkyo* (teaching certificate) system of promotion. Interested senior students must take specific instructor training before a certificate can be awarded.

I interviewed Mr. Shibata on Sunday, 6 September 1998. Mr. Shibata is in his middle seventies. Cancer surgery several years ago has weakened him somewhat, but he still has a keen eye and ear for observing his students. At one point, he stopped our interview because the sound of a bow being used for practice indicated it had been damaged. A young man who had taken his "first shot" that weekend, had overdrawn the bow. Mr. Shibata demanded the offender bring him the bow, whereupon he tapped up and down its whole length, listening to the sound. As it turned out, the bow was intact. "You use too much strength! No good!" he reprimanded the young man, who looked very much like he wished the earth would swallow him up. He was allowed to resume practice, but with a heavier bow.

Mr. Shibata was meticulously dressed in lightweight summer kimono and traditional, pleated trousers (*hakama*), topped off with a broad-brimmed straw hat. The Miyako Kyudojo provided him with a shaded seat from which to observe the "platform"—actually a large rectangle marked out on the grass, with spacers for placement of the kyudoka as they shot at long distance targets at the end of the field.[7] The kyudo practitioners, in their traditional Japanese style clothing, with their deceptively simple-looking bow, were in sharp contrast to the occasional modern Western archers with their compound bows and elaborate sights who also came by to use the field.

INTERVIEW

Q: I heard from Phil Ortiz [New York Tokokyudojo instructor] that you were adopted into the Shibata line, rather than direct lineage. Is that true?

My family point of origin was outside Kagoshima, a small island, maybe Munekazu, I don't know. The first Shibata lived in Tanegashima, but he came from another area so it was difficult rise up in rank in Kagoshima. The samurai of Shimazu, the Satsuma Hatamoto, were very brave, but very isolated, and people from the outside were considered second class, so the first Shibata decided to move to Kyoto, which was then the capital of Japan, in order to be able to move up in rank. At the same time he retained a relationship with the Shimazu in Kagoshima because in Kagoshima there were still good opportunities, so he kept the relationship with the Shimazu. The matter of adoption was that ordinarily, it was boy, boy, boy, not ever girls. But in my case, my mother was the only child born after the 19th generation. My mother died, then there was no one.

Q: So the previous Shibata, the one before you, was your maternal grandfather. Mother's father.

Yes. It is difficult to have all boys generation after generation.

Q: Yes, almost impossible (laughter).

Of course.

Q: Approximately when did your ancestors move to Kyoto?

In the late 16th century. Fifteen hundred something. The location of my house has stayed the same since then.

Q: In the talk on Friday night, you were discussing how kyudo in Japan is now mostly "sport" kyudo. And so the style of kyudo that you now teach and practice has a longer tradition, but the tradition is no longer followed. I wanted your perspective a little bit on how that happened, maybe why you think sport kyudo became so popular in Japan.

Now, young people in Japan are all interested in sport, not meditation. They only practice target shooting, but the target is not the goal. Look at me, my heart is the target. Ego gets cut out . . . cut, cut cut. Many people hope to hit the target—shooting bing, bing, target, target—done. No meditation.

Q: It seems that the Pacific War was the changing point for the change

IN ATTITUDE, OR DO YOU THINK THAT IT BEGAN BEFORE THAT TIME, PERHAPS IN THE 1930'S OR THE 1920'S? WHEN DID SPORT KYUDO BECOME POPULAR?

At the end of the Tokugawa Bakufu, the beginning of the Meiji period [1868–1912]. Later, at the end of the Pacific War, General MacArthur referred to this old style of kyudo as a "fighting style," and started the popular "peace style." But international kyudo [i.e. archery forms around the world] are all fighting styles, but MacArthur and the General Headquarters said "no" to the old style. They made the style so [indicating a change in draw]. That was okay. This Heki system is the samurai old style of kyudo.

Q: YES, GENERAL MACARTHUR CHANGED A GREAT DEAL. . . .

All international archery styles are the same: they are fighting styles. But General Headquarters said "no" to our traditional style, wanting only a "peace style."

Q: NO COMBAT. JUST TARGETS.

Yes, target, target, target.

Q: I WAS WATCHING SOME OF THE WESTERN-STYLE ARCHERS HERE AT THE PUBLIC RANGE, AND I NOTICED ACTUALLY THAT THE ONES WHO ARE SHOOTING—MAYBE THEY SHOOT FOR HUNTING—ARE LEANING TOWARD THE TARGET, WHEREAS THE ONES WHO ARE JUST SHOOTING FOR THE TARGET ARE NOT SHOOTING THAT WAY. SO IT MAY BE TRUE UNIVERSALLY.

Yes.

Q: IN THE IAIDO (ART OF DRAWING THE SWORD) SCHOOL WHERE I PRACTICE, WE DON'T BELONG TO ANY FEDERATION. WE HAVE RANK IN OUR DOJO ONLY BECAUSE OF OUR TEACHER. BECAUSE WE DON'T PARTICIPATE IN ANY ORGANIZATION, OUTSIDE OUR DOJO WE HAVE NOTHING, NO RECOGNITION [LAUGHTER]. BUT MY TEACHER PREFERS THAT RATHER THAN JOIN A FEDERATION. HE THINKS JOINING MAY RUIN THE STYLE. BUT NOW IN THE UNITED STATES AND CANADA FEDERATIONS ARE VERY POPULAR. EVERYONE SEEKS KENDO FEDERATION RANKING.

Kendo and karate are very much the same. Always competition. Go away, go away, go away [making a dismissive gesture].

Q: KYUDO IS VERY ELEGANT.

Soft. But now for everybody in kyudo, the point of shooting has changed to competition.

> SEVEN COORDINATIONS
> 1) *ashibumi* – setting the feet;
> 2) *do zukuri* – setting the body and nocking the arrow;
> 3) *yumi gamae (yugamae)* – orienting the bow towards the target;
> 4) *uchi okoshi* – raising the bow;
> 5) *hiki tori (hikiwake)* –
>   lit. "push-pull," the draw;
> 6) *hanare* – release, and
> 7) *kai* (moment of full extension).

Q: SO, WHEN YOU CAME TO THE UNITED STATES, AND YOU ESTABLISHED A RELATIONSHIP WITH THE SHAMBHALA CENTER....

Twenty years ago I came to meet Shambhala's top teacher, Chogyam Trungpa Rinpoche. I was with my wife. Three or four years later she had an operation—she died. Afterwards, Rinpoche said, "Please stay." I thought about my son-in-law, my family...many, many things. But, I said goodbye to Japan, and I stayed, and picked up Western living [laughter].

Q: SENSEI, WHY DO YOU THINK THAT AMERICANS HAVE AN INTEREST IN MEDITATION AND KYUDO?

Meditation, zazen and other standard forms of meditation are just sitting, which is difficult.

Q: YES, HARD ON YOUR FEET.

Kyudo has "seven coordinations" and you change [takes a position], change, change... Western people find it easier. They're tall and like to stand up.

Q: So Americans like kyudo because they're tall and can stand up [laughter]?

Japanese are short, but Americans are very tall. Stand up mediation is not so difficult. Also, the kyudo kata has lots of changes in it, so it's easier for Americans.

Q: ....because we have no attention span [laughter]. We need entertainment.

Today there are many many machines, and our minds get cloudy. We need to make our minds clear.

Q: This morning, the Western archers came with all of their equipment to practice, compound bows,...

Compound bow?

Q: It's a Western-style bow that has extra cables actually to make it draw easy, very easy [Mr. Shibata laughs out loud]. It is powerful, but it takes no effort. I watched them practice. Then, when they started watching your group, they stopped what they were doing and just watched the kyudo practitioners. I think many Americans like things to be easy.[8]

Yes, yes.

Q: Labor-saving. That's why all the mechanical devices.

Do you know the European archer? With the apple...

Q: Oh, William Tell.

Yes, William Tell.

Q: But that was more difficult, because it was an old style bow.

Now William Tell now looks like the western-style archers....

Q: So kyudo is difficult, I know that because I tried first shot today. For someone who has studied one martial art form and then changes over....

Style only. Not thinking. Heart is the same.

Q: But it's difficult [laughter] for everyone. But why do you think all these people here are interested in doing something that's so difficult?

Yes, it's difficult I think, but a good style. The "seven coordinations" is a good style, and makes a good heart. Natural and good. On the outside, it may be difficult, but inside, not so difficult. Style only is difficult.

Q: So Sensei, how do you see the future of kyudo, not just in this country, but anywhere?

I think it will not grow bigger quickly. If it grows quickly, it will cause damage to the style, but if it grows slowly, slowly, it will expand.

Q: I hope so. My teacher and I have talked about our iaido practice, because now there is much iaido competition. Everyone is trying to take rank and win contests and we never do that, because we think that's not iaido. We do iaido for meditation also, so I asked him, "What happens if everybody leaves, to go for 'sport iaido'? There will be no one left." He said that as long as one person practices, then maybe someone will see them, and then someone will want to learn and then there will be some kind of continuation. One by one.

For samurai, the most important skills were first, the bow, then, horse-riding, then long sword, then, spear. Those were the most important four. Archery and horse riding needed good teachers and much practice. If your teacher died, you didn't have a second one. Without a teacher, learning archery and horse riding was very difficult.

Q: Sensei, is there anything else you'd like to comment about?

To be a student of target shooting is a modern idea. It should be pull, release, sharp cut—cut ego. That's the style. Ego all goes.

Afterword

During some of our informal conversation, Mr. Shibata criticized the ZNKR's standard forms. He suggested kyudo teachers were influenced by SCAP to change the way of orienting the bow towards the target. In the ZNKR style, the bow with the nocked arrow is raised straight up in front of the archer's center line prior to being drawn. In the Heki Bishu Chikurin School, the bow and arrow are positioned forward and more in line with the target. He stated that positioning the bow forward towards the target orients the draw towards a moving target. He suggested the ZNKR change helped eliminate some of the meditative character of kyudo by making it perfectly obvious that the target is the object of practice.

In order to be truly meditative, the practice has to contain some element of a sense of life and death. Philosophically acknowledging a sense of combat helps give Mr. Shibata's kyudo its meditative feel. Though other kyudo teachers emphasize spiritual development and teach traditional styles along with the standard forms, Mr. Shibata maintains that the now-standard shooting style has resulted in the sole interest in "target, target, target" by most contemporary kyudoka in Japan, especially the younger generation. More recently, as interest in kyudo has become more widespread in the West, Mr. Shibata feels competition has eclipsed the meditative aspects here as well.

Mr. Shibata has recently passed his title and responsibilities for bowmaking to his son-in-law, Shibata Kanjuro, who is now the 21st generation headmaster. However, there are few students and the future of the Heki Bishu Chikurin Kyudo School in Japan is somewhat uncertain. Likewise, of the 20 or so "first shot" students at the Miyako Kyudojo Intensive, only a handful will devote serious attention to kyudo. In spite of the difficulties, Mr. Shibata's Western students, and the instructors he has trained, are providing hope for the future of this style of kyudo. Mr. Shibata's style of kyudo is a potent antidote to the competitive rush of everyday life. Hopefully the school will grow, "slowly, slowly" just as Mr. Shibata's predicts.

NOTES

[1] Though *kyudo* is often referred to in English as "Zen archery," the word actually means "way of the bow." Kyudo's relationship to Zen depends to a large extent on how individual teachers approach it. For a detailed discussion of this issue, see Hurst (1998). The seven coordinations of the Heki Bishu Chikurin School roughly coincide with the *hassetsu* (eight stages) of shooting in the Heki Sekka School described in Onuma et al. (1993), though the details of the technique are somewhat different.

[2] "Miyako" means "Capital Tiger," owing to its location in Washington, D.C. All of Shibata Kanjuro's U.S. kyudojo contain the syllable "*ko*" for "tiger" – *Kinko* ("Gold Tiger"), *Kozan* ("Tiger Mountain"), and so on.

[3] The Japanese bow continues in its shamanic function. For example, a bow is twirled at the end of *sumo* tournaments (Moss, 2000, n.p.).

[4] While this is true of many kyudo dojo around the world, Shibata Kanjuro's dojo are somewhat unusual in that they are not affiliated with the ZNKR, nor do they practice the standard forms.

[5] *Rimpoche* is an honorific title meaning "Precious One."

[6] In an example of the sense of religious syncretism found in Japan, Mr. Shibata has no problem teaching Tibetan-style Buddhists kyudo as a meditative practice, even though he is a follower of Shinto himself.

[7] The "platform" marked on the ground represents the layout of traditional kyudo ranges, wherein the archers take their places on an area raised several feet off the ground, with a sheltering roof and one side open to the field, allowing them to shoot in any weather.

[8] This remark related to the presence of compound-bow users who came to the field that day. Many Western archers use traditional weapons in their practice. However, there were none in evidence that weekend.

REFERENCES

ALL NIPPON KYUDO FEDERATION, (1998). Introduction to kyudo. www.bogo.co.uk/kyudo/back.html.

DEPROSPERO, D. AND DEPROSPERO, J. (1996). *Illuminated spirit: conversations with a kyudo master*. New York: Kodansha International.

HARTMAN, E. (1995). Seishinkan Kyudojo: principles of training. www.socrates.berkeley.edu/~cdea/jcac/kyudo/book.html.

HERRIGEL, E. (1953). *Zen in the art of archery*. New York: Vintage Books.

HURST, G. (1998). *Armed martial arts of Japan: Swordsmanship and archery*. New Haven: Yale University Press.

MOSS, H. (2000). Personal communication.

ONUMA, H., DEPROSPERO, D., AND DEPROSPERO, J. (1993). *Kyudo: the essence and practice of Japanese archery*. New York: Kodansha International.

RYUKO KYUDOJO (1992). The seven coordinations. (manuscript).

RYUKO KYUDOJO (1998). Welcome to Ryuko Kyudojo. www.bcn.boulder.co.us/community/ryuko.

SHAMBHALA CENTRE. (2000). Chogyam Trungpa Rinpoche. www.shambhala.org/int/ctrbio.html.

STEIN, H. (1988). *Kyudo: The art of Zen archery*. Longmead: Element Books Ltd.

GLOSSARY

kai	moment of full extension
kyujutsu	bow techniques
yumi	a 7' traditional Japanese long bow
ya	arrow
yumi daoshi	(*yudaoshi*) positioning the bow
yoi	"ready" stance

ACKNOWLEDGMENTS

The author would like to thank Mr. Shibata, the members and teachers of the Miyako Kyudojo and the New York Tokokyudojo, along with Masaoka Eriko, Maeda Etsuko, Philip Ortiz, Laura Jean Ferenz Stewart, and Raymond Sosnowski, for their assistance in preparing this chapter and interview.

chapter 6

Is There a Warrior Within?

by Edwin Symmes, B.A.

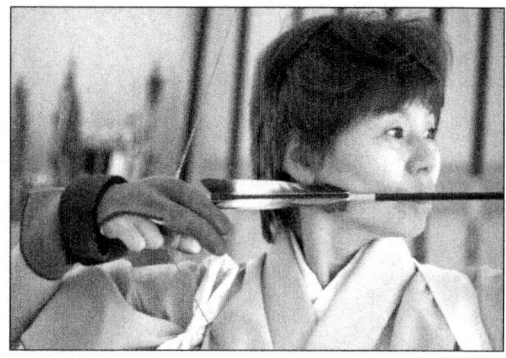

Mrs. Reiko Blackwell, 5th-dan, completes the draw *(kai)*.

The other day a student asked, "Is it appropriate in this day and time for a *kyudo* [archery] practitioner to relate to him- or herself as a warrior?" My first thought was to remember the great "Whiskey Speech" delivered by the late Noah S. "Soggy" Sweat, Jr., former Mississippi legislator, lawyer, and judge, in 1952, when the Mississippi Legislature was considering legalizing liquor.

> ***"The Whiskey Speech"***
> by Noah Sweat, Jr.
>
> My friends, I had not intended to discuss this controversial subject at this particular time. However, I want you to know that I do not shun controversy. On the contrary, I will take a stand on any issue at any time, regardless of how fraught with controversy it might be. You have asked me how I feel about whiskey. All right, here is how I feel about whiskey.

> If when you say whiskey, you mean the devil's brew, the poison scourge, the bloody monster that defiles innocence, dethrones reason, destroys the home, creates misery and poverty, yea, literally takes the bread from the mouths of little children; if you mean the evil drink that topples the Christian man and woman from the pinnacle of righteous, gracious living into the bottomless pit of degradation and despair and shame and helplessness and hopelessness, then certainly I am against it.
>
> But if, when you say whiskey, you mean the oil of conversation, the philosophic wine, the ale that is consumed when good fellows get together, that puts a song in their hearts and laughter on their lips and the warm glow of contentment in their eyes; if you mean Christmas cheer; if you mean the stimulating drink that puts the spring in the old gentleman's step on a frosty, crispy morning; if you mean the drink which enables a man to magnify his joy and his happiness and to forget, if only for a little while, life's great tragedies and heartaches and sorrows; if you mean the drink the sale of which pours into our treasuries untold millions of dollars which are used to provide tender care for our little crippled children, our blind, our deaf, our pitiful aged and infirm. This is my stand, and I will not compromise.

If the concept of a warrior is that of the Mongol Hordes, exceptionally trained warriors who committed such disturbing acts in their conquering of Asia and half of Europe that I prefer to not recount them, then of course the answer is a resounding no!

And that's not double talk.

Fellow instructor Aaron Sensei and I have not used that term. We have used the terms, "martial artist," "follower of the Way of the Bow," and "adherent to the ideals of the Budo Charter."

Let's examine how the Budo Charter challenges us to lead our lives.

Perhaps one of the first enlightenments comes in the first paragraph of the introduction to the Budo Charter in the 2009 publication, *Budo, The Martial Ways of Japan*, published by the Nippon Budokan:

> *Budo*, the Japanese martial ways, have their origins in the age-old martial spirit of Japan. Through centuries of historical and social change, these forms of traditional culture evolved from combat techniques (*jutsu*) into ways of self-discipline (*do*).

The very first paragraph draws a dividing line between what many think of as the traditional martial ways that have to do with combat techniques—i.e.: skills needed by warriors—and the skills employed in modern ways of self-development.

The next two paragraphs:

Seeking the perfect unity of mind and technique, budo has been refined and cultivated into ways of physical training and spiritual development. The study of budo encourages courteous behavior, advances technical proficiency, strengthens the body, and perfects the mind. Modern Japanese have inherited traditional values through budo which continue to play a significant role in the formation of the Japanese personality, serving as sources of boundless energy and rejuvenation. As such, budo has attracted strong interest internationally and is studied around the world.

However, a trend towards infatuation just with technical ability compounded by excessive concern with winning is a severe threat to the essence of budo. To prevent any possible misrepresentation, practitioners of budo must continually engage in self-examination and endeavor to perfect and preserve this traditional culture.

The author readies to shoot at Japan Fest, Atlanta, GA.

Thus we see that the intent has moved away from the combative warrior who focused on the techniques for self and immediate societal preservation. There are many accounts of individual warriors in Japanese and world history. However, in general, the warrior trained diligently to develop technical skills, obey commands, function within the group, and take on a leadership role when required.

The samurai warriors from whom the budo code developed, established the ways that became fixed in the letter and the spirit of the Budo Charter. The following is the 2004 English-language version as updated from the original establishment document from April 23, 1987, by the Japanese Budo Association.

ARTICLE 1: Objective of Budo
Through physical and mental training in the Japanese martial ways, budo exponents seek to build their character, enhance their sense of judgment, and become disciplined individuals capable of making contributions to society at large.

ARTICLE 2: Training (*Keiko*)
When training in budo, practitioners must always act with respect and courtesy, adhere to the prescribed fundamentals of the art, and resist the temptation to pursue mere technical skill, rather than strive towards the perfect unity of mind, body, and technique.

ARTICLE 3: Competition (*Shiai*)
Whether competing in a match or doing a set of forms (*kata*), exponents must externalize the spirit underlying budo. They must do their best at all times, winning with modesty, accepting defeat gracefully and constantly exhibiting self-control.

ARTICLE 4: Training Hall (*Dojo*)
The dojo is a special place for training the mind and body. In the dojo, budo practitioners must maintain discipline and show proper courtesies and respect. The dojo should be a quiet, clean, safe, and solemn environment.

ARTICLE 5: Teaching
Teachers of budo should always encourage others to also strive to better themselves and diligently train their minds and bodies, while continuing to further their understanding of the technical principles of budo. Teachers should not allow focus to be put on winning or losing in competition, or on technical ability alone. Above all, teachers have a responsibility to set an example as role models.

ARTICLE 6: Promoting Budo
Persons promoting budo must maintain an open-minded and international perspective as they uphold traditional values. They should make efforts to

contribute to research and teaching, and do their utmost to advance budo in every way.

Top, left: Aaron Blackwell, 6th-dan. Right: Archers shoot in turn during a rotation. Bottom: Five-person testing in the Simpsonville, SC, Kyudojo.

Thus we have a basis for deciding personally if we want to follow the Budo Way or not. To do so, we must train diligently both the body and the mind to become more disciplined, to enhance character, and to hone judgment. During this training, we must always be respectful—not do our own thing—and practice the proper techniques. In the case of kyudo, we must constantly fight the seductiveness of the target and relinquish the short-term gratification of just hitting the *mato* to the longer-term, much more mature satisfaction of using proper technique that will result in the hit.

During a demonstration of kyudo an audience member shouted out, "When are you going to kill something with that thing?" The Buddhist priest I was demonstrating with answered, "The aim of kyudo is to kill one's own ego."

It is not easy.

The author demonstrates at Japan Fest, Atlanta, GA.

When the body, mind, and spirit are equally trained, a harmony of being is realized that provides the living role model for students. This is the goal we should strive for. If we stop at anything less, we will not have fully realized our personal potential. Therefore, our students will achieve less than their potential.

To me, the greatest compliment for teachers is to have their students surpass them. In order to do that, students must absorb all that they can from the teacher, plus do their own personal research into the Way of their choice. Then they may eventually make the forms so deeply ingrained that they emerge as a unified whole, adding to the knowledge and beauty of this most unusual, challenging, and rewarding life-long path we have chosen.

Thus, the conclusion regarding the concept of whether it is appropriate for a person to be a "warrior" in today's society is this: If the warrior follows the high calling of the Budo Charter, then it is not only appropriate, it is a requisite.

CREDIT
Photographs by Aaron Blackwell,
Edwin Symmes, Yoshiya Furuta and Jan Isley.
Copyright 2009 the Kyudo Alliance.

chapter 7

Sword-Cutting Practice of Feudal Japan: Anatomical Considerations of Tameshigiri

by Peter J. Ward, Ph.D.

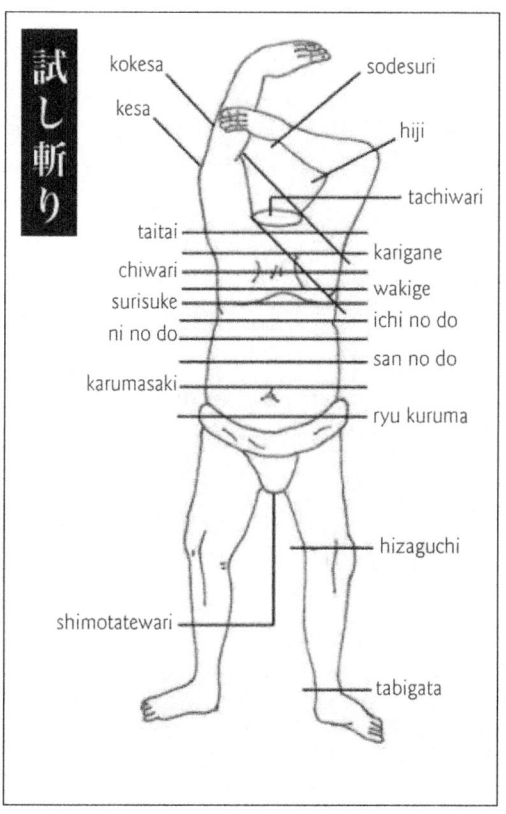

Figure 1: This diagram demonstrates the placement of each cut on the body during tameshigiri.

Introduction

Tameshigiri, or test cutting, was extensively practiced in feudal Japan. While stationary objects were often used in this practice, it was common to use the bodies of executed criminals to test the cutting abilities of swords and the swordsmen themselves. In this practice, the body was taken to an area containing a mount of sand that was built with bamboo poles projecting upward. The sand mound and poles were used to position the body so a powerful stroke could be delivered to specific targets.

Tameshigiri was relatively common during the era preceding the Warring States period (starting in the sixteenth century) of Japan and is documented as having been extensively practiced by members of the samurai class during the seventeenth century. At that time, Japan was united under a single military leader, the shogun Tokugawa Ieyasu. Under the Tokugawa shogunate there were fewer armed conflicts within Japan, and tameshigiri was used as a way to maintain the "warrior spirit" of the samurai. The practice remained widespread within the samurai class into the eighteenth century. During the eighteenth century, as the samurai class transitioned from full-time warriors to bureaucrats, the grotesque aspects of tameshigiri clashed with the more elegant persona of the samurai civil servant.

Tameshigiri was used primarily to grade the quality of blades that were produced by swordsmiths. Despite no longer being at war, the paired swords (one long *katana* and one shorter *wakizashi*) remained the symbol of the samurai class, and their quality was of great concern. During this time, tameshigiri was left to a select group of lower-status samurai who were professional blade testers. This role often remained within specific family lineages, such as the Yamada family. The practice continued into the nineteenth century, until the whole social strata of Japan was reordered by the Meiji Restoration in 1868. The practice of tameshigiri on the bodies of executed criminals ceased at this time (Joy and Hogitaro, 1963; Kremer, 2008; Takeuchi, 2009).

Objectives of This Study

The historical records related to tameshigiri primarily list the early high status samurai who conducted the practice, the professional sword testers who inherited it, and the executed criminals upon whose bodies the cuts were delivered. Little information has been presented on the cuts themselves. The purpose of this study is to use original diagrams that detail the cuts and correlate them with the anatomical structures that would have been encountered by a blade as it passed through the body. This study will list the structures involved in each tameshigiri cut and conjecture on the factors that contributed to the difficulty of each cut.

Methods

The name, placement, and difficulty of each cut were taken from the seminal work on this topic in English (Joly and Hogitaro, 1963) and are shown in figure 1 (See first page of this chapter). The Yamada family, a lineage of professional *suemonoshi* (test cutters), listed the difficulty of each cut. In order of increasing difficulty, the cuts are as follows:

1) sodesuri (figure 2)
2) tabigata (figure 3)
3) kokesa (figure 4)
4) ichi no do (figure 5)
5) ni no do (figure 6)
6) san no do (figure 7)
7) shimotateware (not pictured)
8) suritsuke (figure 8)
9) kurumasaki (figure 9)
10) wakige (figure 10)
11) tachiwari (figure 11)
12) kesa (figure 12)
13) chiwari (figure 13)
14) karigane (figure 14)
15) taitai (figure 15)
16) ryo kuruma (figure 16)

The Visible Human slice viewer (http://visiblehuman) was accessed to create a "slice" that replicated each of the cuts from the Joly and Hogitaro text. Once the images were harvested, the structures were identified and labeled.

Shimotatewari was not pictured. This exclusion was not out of squeamishness but because the extent of the cut was unclear. It might involve only the genitalia or might have been a sagittal cut of the pelvic bones. Given its placement in the list, the latter is more likely, but its exact dimensions are unknown. Two cuts present on the illustration (figure 1) were not listed, images of these two cuts, *hiji* (figure 17) and *hizaguchi* (figure 18), were gathered in the same way as the listed cuts.

Results

The thickest sections such as taitai (figure 15) and karigane (figure 14) all tended to be among the most difficult cuts. Not surprisingly, the smaller sections such as sodesuri (figure 2) and tabigata (figure 3) were the two least difficult cuts. However, it is also clear that the bony content of the cut is of prime importance. For example, the most difficult cut, ryu kuruma (figure 16), is very similar in size and soft-tissue composition to kurumasaki (figure 9). However, ryu kuruma contains a significant amount of bone, while kurumasaki contains a single lumbar vertebra. Therefore, bony content is also determinant of the difficulty of each cut. This is in agreement with a forensic investigation of historical battleground remains showing that battlefield cuts were frequently deflected by bone (Karasulas, 2004).

FIGURE 1: This diagram demonstrates the placement of each cut on the body during tameshigiri. See the first page of this chapter for reference.

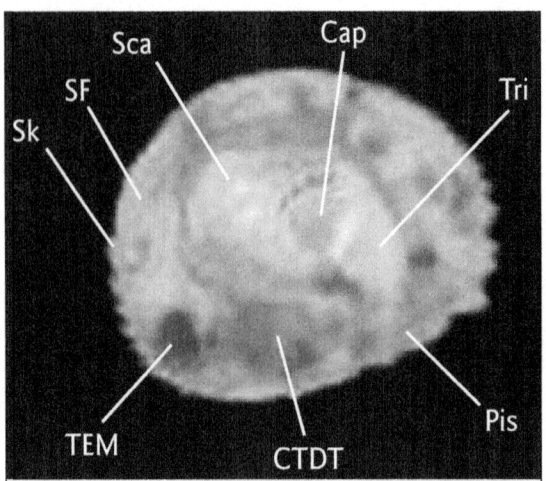

FIGURE 2: Sodesuri (wrist). Structures encountered —
Cap: capitate
CTDT: carpal tunnel and digital flexor tendons
Pis: pisiform
Sca: scaphoid
SF: subcutaneous fat
Sk: skin
TEM: thenar eminence muscles
Tri: triquetrum

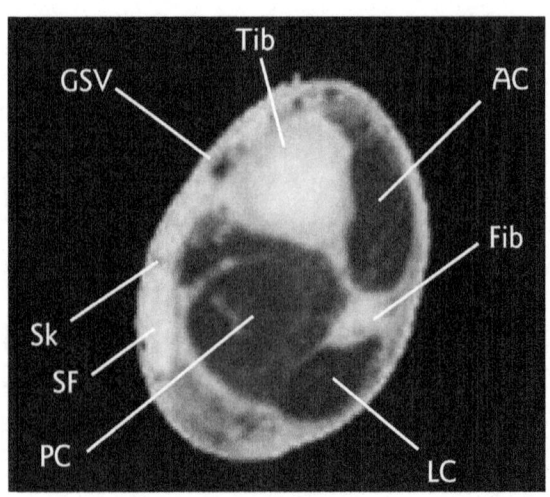

FIGURE 3: Tabigata (ankle). Structures encountered —
AC: anterior compartment of leg
Fib: fibula
GSV: greater saphenous vein
LC: lateral compartment of leg
PC: posterior compartment of leg
SF: subcutaneous fat
Sk: skin
Tib: tibia

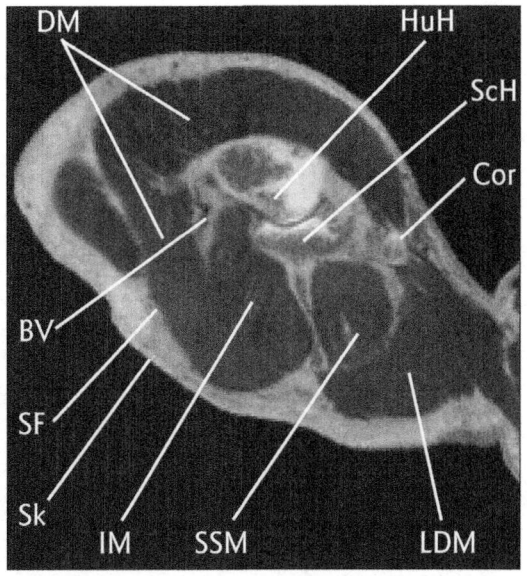

FIGURE 4: Kokesa. Structures encountered —
BV: brachial vessels
Cor: coracoid process
    of scapula
HuH: humeral head
IM: infraspinatus muscle
LDM: latissius dorsi muscle
ScH: scapular head
Sk: skin
SSM: subscapularis muscle

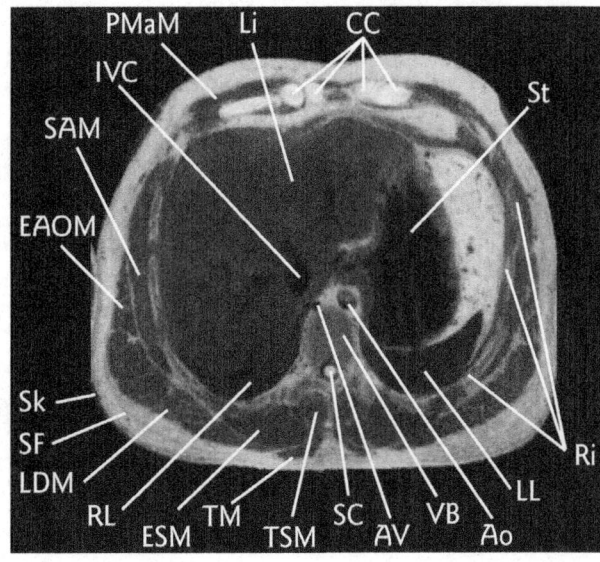

FIGURE 5: Ichi no do. Structures encountered —
Ao: aorta
AV: azygos vein
CC: costal cartilages
EAOM: external abdominal oblique muscle
ESM: erector spinae muscle
IVC: inferior vena cava
LDM: latissimus dorsi muscle
Li: liver
LL: left lung
PMaM: pectoralis major muscle
Ri: ribs
RL: right lung
SAM: serratus anterior muscle
SC: spinal canal
SF: subcutaneous fat
Sk: skin
Sto: stomach
TM: trapezius muscle
TSM: transversospinalis muscles
VB: vertebral body

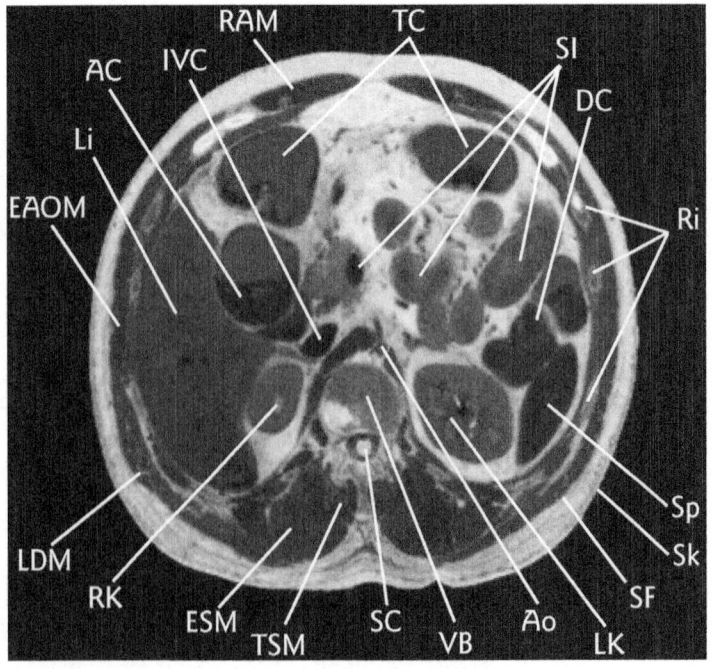

FIGURE 6: Ni no do. Structures encountered —
AC: ascending colon
Ao: aorta
DC: descending colon
EAOM: external abdominal oblique muscle
ESM: erector spinae muscle
IVC: inferior vena cava
LDM: latissimus dorsi muscle
Li: liver
LK: left kidney
RAM: rectus abdominis muscle
Ri: ribs
RK: right kidney
SC: spinal canal
SF: subcutaneous fat
SI: small intestines
Sk: skin
Sp: splean
TC: transverse colon
TSM: transversospinalis muscles
VB: vertebral body

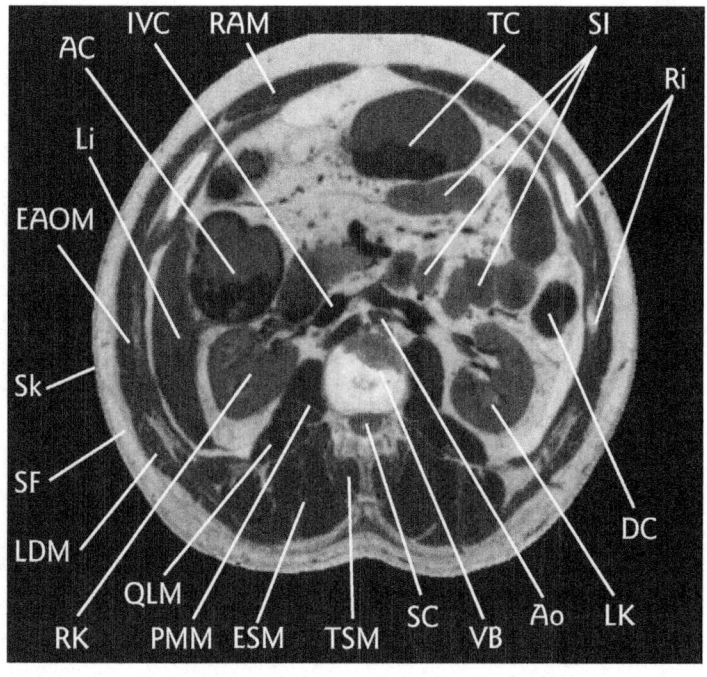

FIGURE 7: San no do. Structures encountered —
AC: ascending colon
Ao: aorta
DC: descending colon
EAOM: external abdominal oblique muscle
ESM: erector spinae muscle
IVC: inferior vena cava
LDM: latissius dorsi muscle
Li: liver
LK: left kidney
QLM: quadrattus lumborum muscle
PMM: psoa major muscle
RAM: rectus abdominis muscle
Ri: ribs
RK: right kidney
SC: spinal canal
SF: subcutaneous fat
SI: small intestines
Sk: skin
TC: transverse colon
TSM: transversospinalis muscles
VB: vertebral body (includes portion of internalvertebral disc)

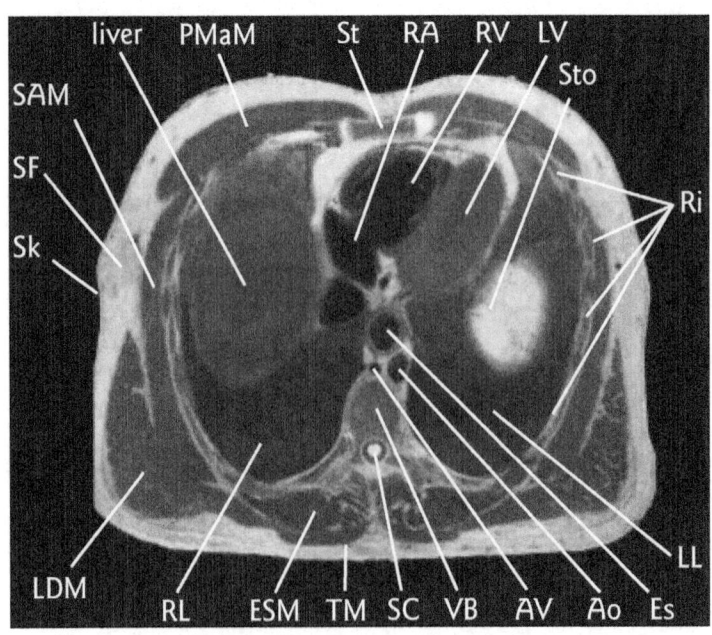

FIGURE 8: Suritsuke. Structures encountered —
Ao: aorta
AV: azygos vein
Es: esophagus
LDM: latissimus dorsi muscle
LL: left lung
LV: left ventricle
PMaM: pectoralis major muscle
RA: right atrium
Ri: ribs
RL: right lung
RV: right ventricle
SAM: serratus anterior muscle
SC: spinal canal
SF: subcutaneous fat
Sk: skin
St: sternum
Sto: stomach
TM: trapezius muscle
VB: vertebral body

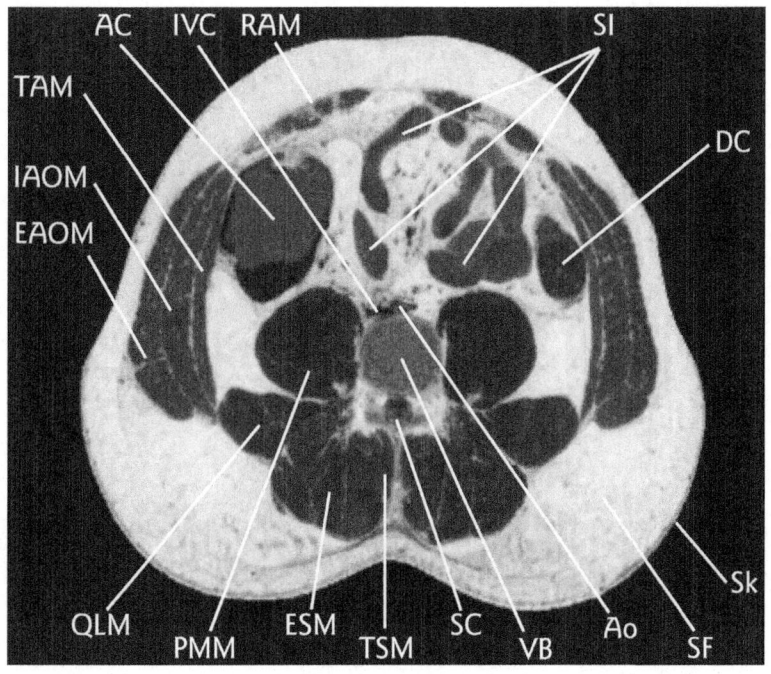

FIGURE 9: Structures encountered —
AC: ascending colon
Ao: aorta
DC: descending colon
EAOM: external abdominal oblique muscle
ESM: erector spinae muscle
IAOM: internal abdominal oblique muscle
IVC: inferior vena cava
QLM: quadrattus lumborum muscle
PMM: psoas major muscle
RAM: rectus abdominis muscle
SC: spinal canal
SF: subcutaneous fat
SI: small intestines
Sk: skin
TAM: transversus abdominis muscle
TSM: transversospinalis muscles
VB: vertebral body

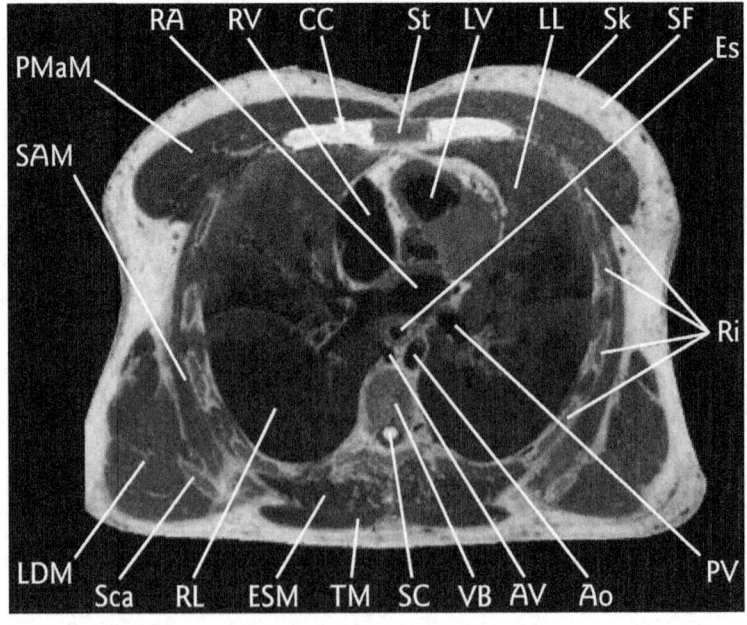

FIGURE 10: Wakige. Structures encountered —

Ao: aorta
AV: azygos vein
CC: costal cartilage
Es: esophagus
ESM: erector spinae muscles
LL: left ventricle
PMaM: pectoralis major muscle
PV: pulmonary vessels
RA: right atrium
Ri: ribs
RL: right lung
RV: right ventricle
SAM: serratus anterior muscle
SC: spinal canal
Sca: scapula
SF: subcutaneous fat
Sk: skin
St: sternum
TM: trapezius muscle
VB: vertebral body

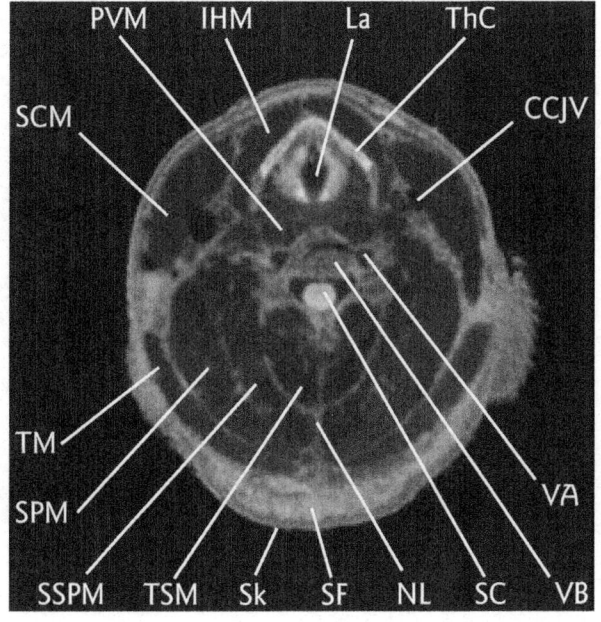

FIGURE 11: Tachiwari. Structures encountered —
CCJV: common carotid artery and jugular vein
IHM: infrahyoid muscles
La: larynx
NL: nuchal ligament
PVM: prevertebral muscles
SC: spinal canal
SCM: sternocleidomastoid muscle
SF: subcutaneous fat
Sk: skin
SPM: splenius muscles
SSPM: semispinalis muscles
SVC: superior vena cava
ThC: thyroid cartilage
TM: trapezius muscle
Tr: trachea
TSM: transversospinalis muscles
A: vertebral artery
VB: vertebral body

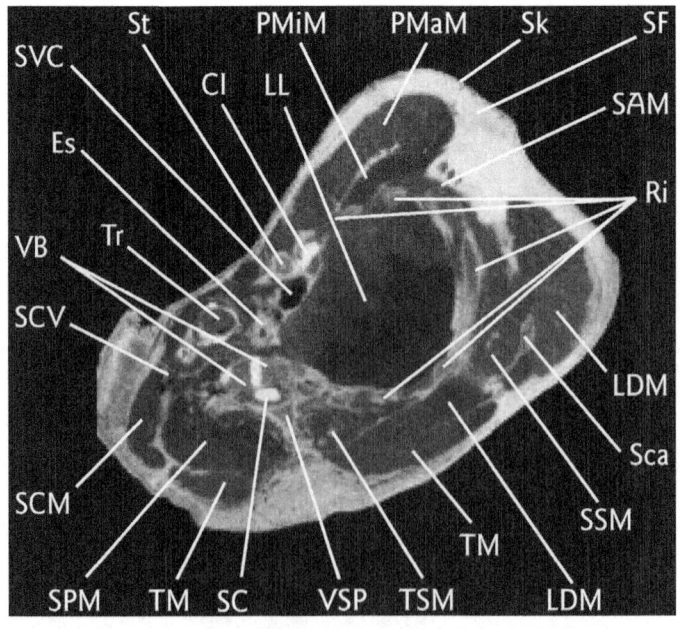

FIGURE 12: Kesa. Structures encountered —
Cl: clavicle
Es: esophagus
LDM: latissimus dorsi muscle
LL: left lung
PMaM: pectoralis major muscle
PMiM: pectoralis minor muscle
Ri: ribs
SAM: serratus anterior muscle
SC: spinal canal
Sca: scapula
SCV: subclavian vessels
SF: subcutaneous fat
Sk: skin
SPM: splenius muscles
SSM: subscapularis muscle
St: sternum
SVC: superior vena cava
TM: trapezius muscle
TSM: transversospinalis muscles
Tr: trachea
VB: vertebral bodies
VSP: vertebral spinous process

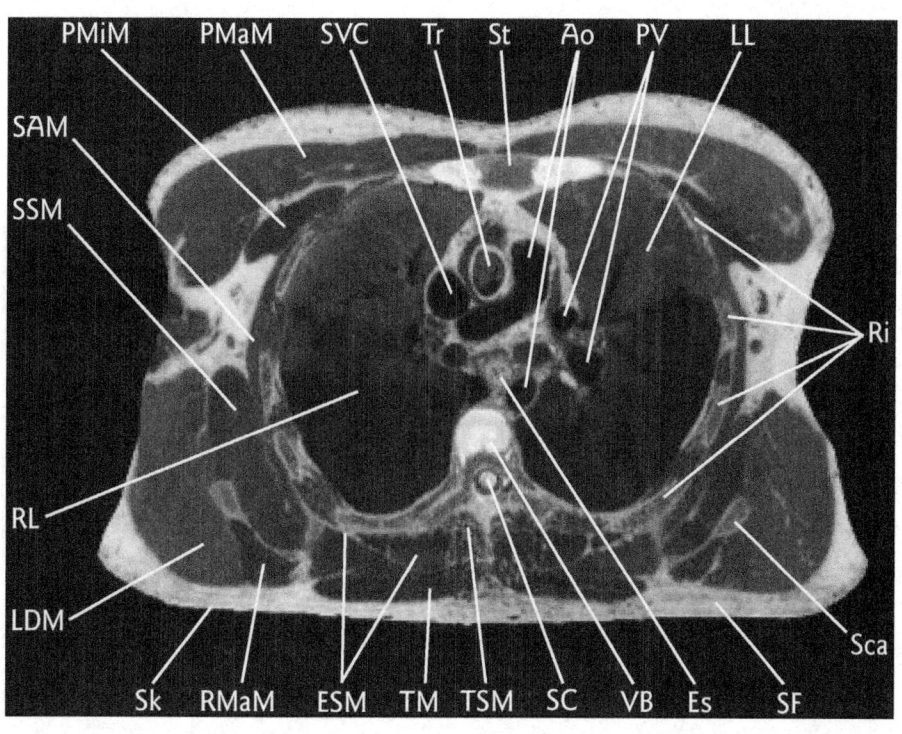

FIGURE 13: Chiwari. Structures encountered —

Ao: aorta
Es: esophagus
ESM: erector spinae muscles
LDM: latissimus dorsi muscle
LL: left lung
PMaM: pectoralis major muscle
PMiM: pectoralis minor muscle
PV: pulmonary vessels
Ri: ribs
RL: right lung
RMaM: rhomboid major muscle
SAM: serratus anterior muscle
SC: spinal canal
Sca: scapula
SF: subcutaneous fat
Sk: skin
SSM: subscapularis muscle
St: sternum
SVC: superior vena cava
TM: trapezius muscle
Tr: trachea
TSM: transversospinalis muscles
VB: vertebral body

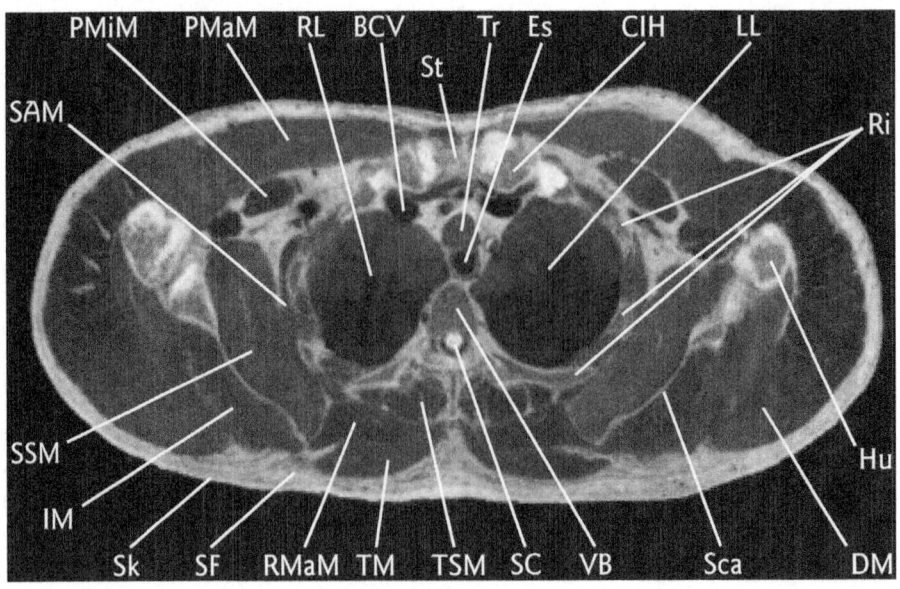

FIGURE 14: Karigane. Structures encountered —
BCV: brachiocephalic vessels
CIH: clavicular head
DM: deltoid muscle
Es: esophagus
Hu: humerus
IM: infraspinatus muscle
LL: left lung
PMaM: pectoralis major muscle
PMiM: pectoralis minor muscle
Ri: ribs
RL: right lung
RMaM: rhomboid major muscle
SAM: serratus anterior muscle
SC: spinal canal
Sca: scapula
SF: subcutaneous fat
Sk: skin
SSM: subscapularis muscle
St: sternum
TM: trapezius muscle
Tr: trachea
TSM: transversospinalis muscles
VB: vertebral body

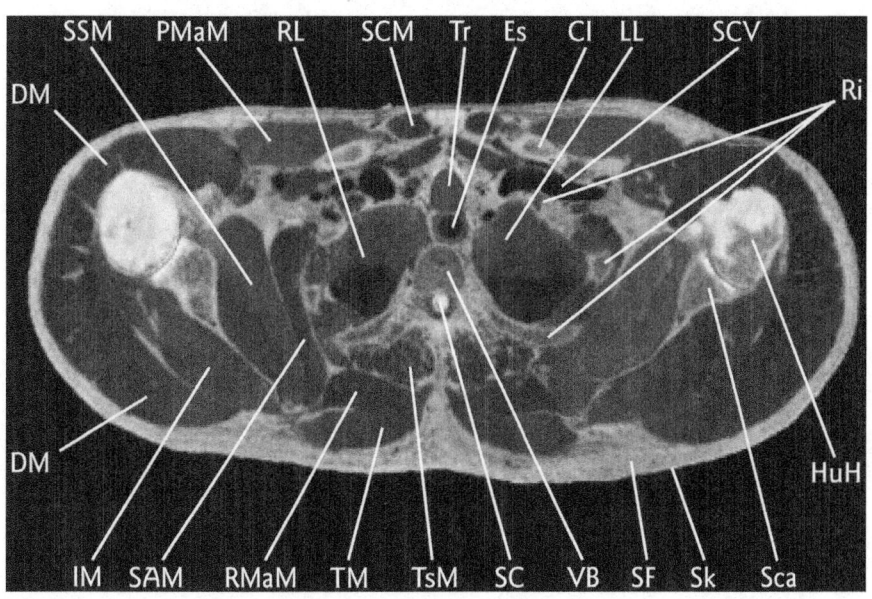

FIGURE 15: Taitai. Structures encountered —
Cl: clavicle
DM: deltoid muscle
Es: esophagus
HuH: humeral head
IM: infraspinatus muscle
LL: left lungs
PMaM: pectoralis major muscle
Ri: ribs
RL: right lung
RMaM: rhomboid major muscle
SAM: serratus anterior muscle
SC: spinal canal
Sca: scapula
SCM: sternocleidomastoid muscle
SCV: subclavian vessels
SF: subcutaneous fat
Sk: skin
SSM: subscapularis muscle
TM: trapezius muscle
Tr: trachea
TSM: transversospinalis muscles
VB: vertebral body

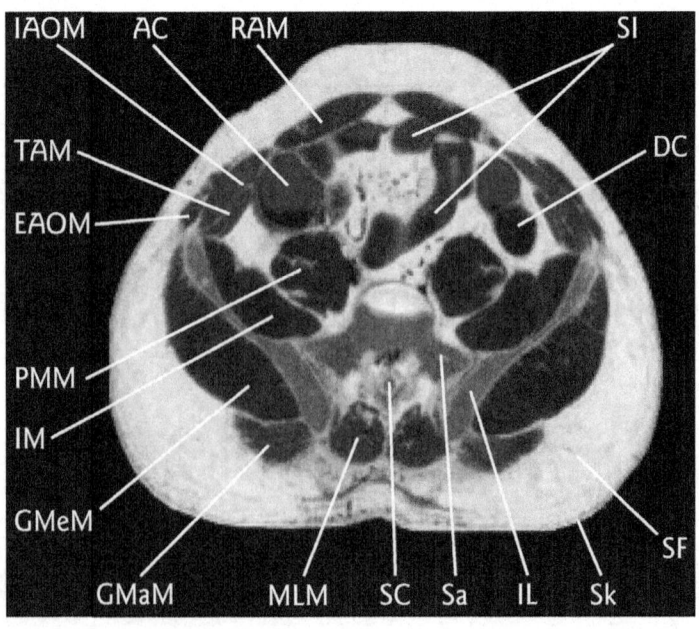

FIGURE 16: Ryo kuruma. Structures encountered —
AC: ascending colon
DC: descending colon
EAOM: external abdominal oblique muscle
GMaM: gluteus maximus muscle
GMeM: gluteus medius muscle
IAOM: internal abdominal oblique muscle
IL: ilium
IM: iliacus muscle
MLM: multifidis lumborum muscle
PMM: psoas major muscle
RAM: rectus abdominis muscle
Sa: sacrum
SC: spinal canal
SI: small intestines
SF: subcutaneous fat
Ski: skin
TAM: transversus abdominis muscle

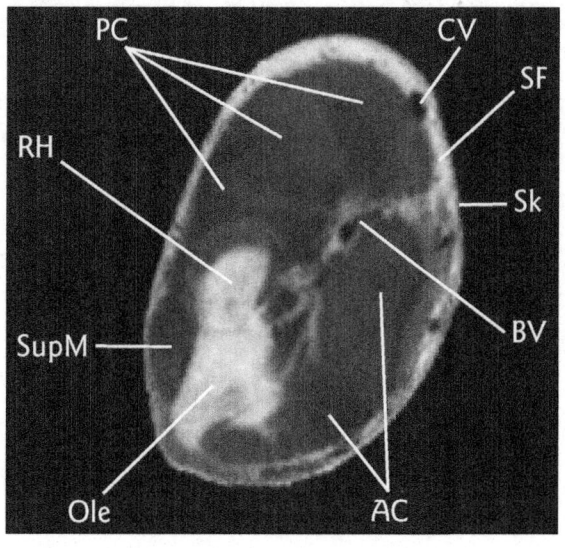

FIGURE 17: Hiji. Structures encountered —
AC: anterior compartment of forearm
BV: brachial vessels
CV: cephalic vein
Ole: olecranon process of ulna
PC; posterior compartment of forearm
RH: radial head
SF: subcutaneous fat
Sk: skin
SupM: supinator muscle

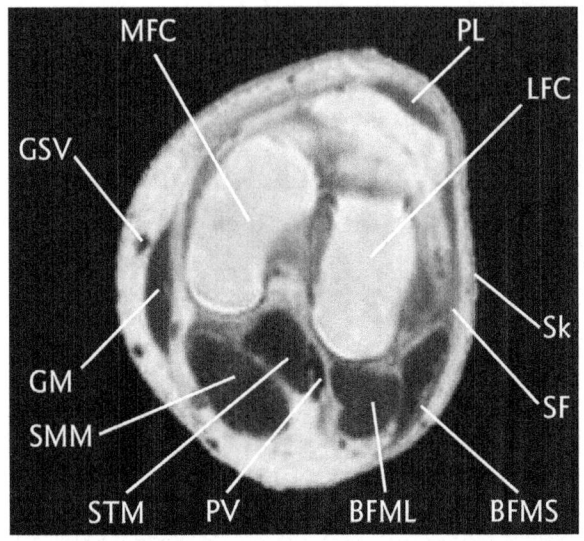

FIGURE 18: Hizaguchi. Structures encountered —
BML: biceps femoris muscle, long head
BMS: biceps femoris muscle, short head
GM: gracilis muscle
GSV: greater saphenous vein
LFC: lateral femoral condyle
MFC: medial femoral condyle
PL: patellar ligament
PV: popliteal vessels
SF: subcutaneous fat
Sk: skin
SMM: semimembranosus muscle
STM: semitendinosus muscle

Concluding Remarks

Tameshigiri cuts that were listed as difficult were thick and had a significant amount of bony tissue. This makes intuitive sense, since thicker targets have more tissue to impede the sword, and bone can deflect a blade. The mystique that has grown around the samurai swords in popular culture obscures the fact that these blades are not able to effortlessly cleave people in half. A forensic review of samurai bones from the Zaimokuza battlefield shows that even these feudal warriors were unable to consistently make clean cuts through their opponents. Evidence of bony deflection and "skipping" of a blade across tissues was found repeatedly (Karasulas, 2004). While these deflected cuts would still have been associated with massive soft-tissue trauma, it is clear that practices like tameshigiri were necessarily intended to sharpen the skill of those involved.

As the tameshigiri use of enemy combatants or executed criminals waned, inanimate objects took their place. It is still common practice in many *kenjutsu* (combative study of the Japanese sword) schools to cut rice stalk bales soaked with water and wrapped around a bamboo pole to mimic a limb. Even in this process it takes practice to deliver a clean cut that is not deflected by the bamboo within the target (Karasulas, 2004). The tameshigiri cuts that replicate the difficulty of these sorts of cuts are hizaguchi, hiji, sodesuri, and tabigata. The Yamada family considered these to be relatively simple in comparison to the cuts that passed through a larger cross section of the body. The most difficult cuts, ryo kuruma and tai-tai, involve cleaving through a large section of the body with a significant core of dense bone. The irregular shape of these bones may also make a clean cut exceedingly difficult.

Much as the samurai class lost interest in the practice of tameshigiri on the bodies of executed criminals, modern readers may find this to be a brutal and grotesque practice. Apart from the unavoidable gore, the idea of destroying a human body in such a manner is repugnant to many. Because the bodies of condemned criminals were used during these sessions, tameshigiri was also seen as an additional punishment to the criminal, since his body could no longer be properly buried. Samurai, clergy, women, and those with visible skin conditions were typically exempted.

Before delivering a verdict on the morality of this practice, modern readers should place tameshigiri into its proper historical and cultural context. Unlike anatomical dissection, the purpose of this practice was not an understanding of the human body for education or discovery. It was intended to test the ability of swords and swordsmen to cut effectively in a militarized and violent time. While this practice might have been a preface to a more modern understanding of human anatomy, this development did not occur. Instead, the social pressures in historical Japan pushed the development of tameshigiri to become a way of measuring the prestige of a hand-forged blade. A modern appreciation of scientific anatomy was ushered in with the Meiji Restoration of 1868, the same time as tameshigiri of corpses ceased and Japan entered a period of intense modernization.

ACKNOWLEDGMENTS

I would like to thank the National Library of Medicine and the Visible Human Project for creating the images and data at the heart of this project. This would have been impossible without Professor R.D. Hersch and team of the Ecole Polytechnique Fédérale de Lausanne (EPFL). Switzerland, who developed the Visible Human viewer and have made it available for use in scientific investigations. More important, I would like to acknowledge the visual male himself, Joseph Paul Jernigan.

BIBLIOGRAPHY

BERENSON, A. (2005, October 15). Lipitor or generic? Billion-dollar battle looms. *New York Times*. Also found at http://www.nytimes.com/2005/10/15/business/15statin.html?pagewanted=all.

JOLY, H., AND HOGITARO, I. (1963). *The sword and same*. Boston: Charles Tuttle.

KARASULAS, A. (2004). Zaimokuza reconsidered: The forensic evidence and classical Japanese swordsmanship. *World archaeology*, 36(4): 507–518.

Kremer, C., Racette, S., Schellenberg, M., Chaltchi, A., and Sauvageau, A. (2008). *American Journal of Forensic Medicine and Pathology*, 29(1): 5–8.

Takeuchi, S. (2009). Tameshigiri (and suemonogiri) as a sub-cultural custom and social structure in feudal era Japan: A socio-cultural analysis of transformation of its symbolic meanings and functions. *Asian Social Science*, 5 (11): 3–14.

Visible Human Slice Viewer. Courtesy Prof. R. Hersch, Ecole Polytechnique Federale de Lausanne (EPFL), Switzerland, Visible Human Web Server http://visiblehuman.epfl.ch. Accessed December 1, 2011.

index

All Japan Kyudo Federation, 1
Anahachiman Shrine, 35
Anazawa-ryu Naginatajutsu, 25
Araki-ryu, 19, 22
archery (*kyudo*), 1-3, 30, 50-51, 55, 58, 59 note 1, 61
archery shooting kata, 2-3
archery testing, 1-3, 65
aristocratic warrior class (*bushi*), 8, 19, 25-27, 35, 51
Asakuma (shihan), 2, 4
ax-blade naginata (*nata-naginata*), 12-13
Baker, Edward, 2
bisento blade, 11, 27
blade parts, 15
bow, 2, 8, 19, 30, 34-35, 37, 39, 49-53, 56-58, 59 notes 1 and 3
budo, 1, 3, 5-6, 52-53, 62-65
Budo Charter, 62, 64, 66
Budokan, 5, 62
Cauley, Thomas, 2
chain and sickle, 4, 41
Choku Gen-ryu, 23-25
competition, 51, 56, 58-59, 64
dagger, 26
distance (*maai*), 44
Draeger, Donn, 8
Edo Castle, 33
guan-dao/shang-dao, 10-12, 27 note 2
Hagenaer, Hendrick, 30, 38
hand guard (*tsuba*), 16, 19-20
Heki Bishu Chikurin School, 50, 53, 58-59, 59 note 1
Higashi, Tomoko, 24
Higo Ko-ryu, 19
Shiradori, Ichiko, 23
hoko spear, 8-9, 13
horse, 8-9, 18-19, 26, 30-35, 37, 39, 51, 58
iaido, 41, 56, 58
Ikkaku-ryu Juttejutsu, 41

Isshin-ryu Kusarigamajutsu, 41
Isshin-ryu, 25
Ittatsu-ryu Hojojutsu, 41
Iwami no kami Masanari, 36
Japan Jodo Association, 42, 48 note 3
Japanese Budo Association, 64
Japanese Polearms, 15
kendo, 24, 41, 51, 56
Jikishin Kage-ryu Naginata-do, 24
jodo, 1, 6, 41-42, 47
  testing, 4-5
judo, 52
jutte or *sai*, 41
Kano, Jigoro, 52
karate, 2, 56
Kasai Denyemon Kanyu, 23
Kashima Shinto-ryu, 19
Kashima, Susumu, 9
Kasumi Shinto-ryu, 41
kenjutsu, 41, 85
Keyserling, Hans Jurgen, 32-33, 39 note 7
kihon (fundamentals), 42-44, 47
kiai, 3-4
kyudo, 50-59, 59 notes 1, 6, and 7, 61, 65
MacArthur, Douglas, 55
Megata, Morito, 33
Miyamoto, Musashi, 2, 4
Miura Gorozaburo, 39
Miyako Kyudojo, 50, 53, 59-60
Mongols, 24, 62
monks (*sohei*), 8, 27
mounted archery (*kyuba*), 8-9, 30, 32-37
Muso-ryu, 1-2, 4
nagamaki, 18-20, 23
naginata construction, 16
Naginata Renmei, 24
Ogasawara School, 36-37, 51
Ogasawara Heibei Tsuneharu, 33-34
Komai, Toshimasa, 35
Ono-ha Itto-ryu, 23

Ortiz, Phil, 54
Otofuji, Ichizo, 5
pull and drop strike, 41-46
Ran Ai jo kata (Harmony Out of Chaos), 4
ridgeline (*shinogi*), 17-21
samurai, 5, 7, 51, 54-55, 58, 64, 68, 85-86
Saotome, Mitsugi, 2
Sasamori, Junzo, 24
Secret Book of Mounted Archery of the Ogasawara School, 37
seven coordinations of kyudo, 50, 56-57, 59 note 1
Shibata, Kanjuro, 49-50, 52, 59 note 4
Shimizu, Takaji, 42
Shin Gyo To-ryu, 22
Shindo Muso-ryu Jodokai, 1
shodan, 1-5
Shosoin, 9-10
spear (*yari*), 8-9, 11, 22-25, 58
stone stabber (*ishizuki*), 16-17
strategy, 9
Suigetsu jo kata (Moon in The Water), 4
sumo, 26, 59 note 3
tachi sword, 8-9, 11, 19

teaching, 4, 6, 25, 37, 42, 53, 59 note 6, 64-65
teboko blade, 9-10
Tenshin Shoden Katori Shinto-yu, 22
test cutting (*tameshigiri*), 67-68, 85-86
test cutting difficulty, 68-69, 85
Tibetan Buddhism, 53, 59
Toda-ha Buko-ryu, 19
Tokugawa, Ieyasu, 25, 68
Tokyo National Museum, 9
Toyotomi, Hideyori, 25
track (*sakuri*), 30, 32, 35, 37
training, 2-6, 22, 25-26, 36, 42, 50, 53, 63-65
training hall (*dojo*), 2, 4, 6, 56, 64
Tsuki Zue (Standing Stick) jo kata, 4
Tsurugaoka Hachimangu Shrine, 29
tying (*hojojutsu*), 41
Uchida-ryu, 41
Uesugi, Kenshin, 19
Visible Human, 69
yabusame, 29-30, 32-38, 39 note 2
Yoshimune (*shogun*), 29-38
Zaimokuza battlefield, 85
Zen Nihon Kyudo Renmei, 51

Notes

Printed in Great Britain
by Amazon

63259796R00057